THE FACE OF RESISTANCE

*Aung San Suu Kyi
and Burma's Fight for Freedom*

AUNG ZAW

MEKONG PRESS

To the political prisoners in Burma

MEKONG PRESS was initiated in 2005 by Silkworm Books with the financial support of the Rockefeller Foundation. In 2007, the Mekong Press Foundation was registered as a nonprofit organization to encourage and support the work of local scholars, writers, and publishing professionals in Cambodia, Laos, Vietnam, and the other countries in the Greater Mekong Subregion. Books published by Mekong Press (www.mekongpress.com) are marketed and distributed internationally. Mekong Press also holds seminars and training workshops on different aspects of book publishing, and helps find ways to overcome some of the huge challenges faced by small book publishers in the region.

ISBN: 978-616-215-066-1

Published in 2013 by
Mekong Press
6 Sukkasem Road, T. Suthep
Chiang Mai 50200 Thailand
info@mekongpress.com
http://www.mekongpress.com

Cover photo from Reuters

Typeset in Candara 9.5 pt. by Silk Type

Printed in Thailand by O. S. Printing House, Bangkok

5 4 3 2 1

CONTENTS

ACKNOWLEDGMENTS

First and foremost, I am grateful to my colleagues at *The Irrawaddy*. They have always given me moral support as well as understanding when I took a few months leave to finish work on this book. They all made sure *The Irrawaddy* continued to flow.

I would like to thank my old friends who remained inside Burma while I was in exile, particularly the members of the Insein Sarpay Wine literary discussion group, founded in the Rangoon suburb of Insein in 1987, the year before the nationwide pro-democracy uprising. Many of them were many years my elder, and I always looked to them for inspiration and the strength that I needed to continue the long journey of my self-imposed exile. In my longing to go home, I often met and reunited with them in my dreams. They opened my eyes and urged me to try to understand the dark side of my country and the nature of the military and authoritarian rulers. I cannot forget fellow members of the underground cell that I belonged to in Burma, some of whom endured long jail sentences. Despite the hardships they suffered, they never lost their hope of achieving freedom and democracy in Burma. They are my heroes.

Returning to my homeland in January 2012 for the first time in twenty-four years, I was able to have frank and candid discussions with many who remained inside Burma. Of these, I would like to thank Daw Aung San Suu Kyi, Hkun Htun Oo, U Win Tin, U Tin Oo, Min Ko Naing, Ko Ko Gyi, and many other activists and former political prisoners involved in the democracy movement. I would like to thank the senior journalists and writers Maung Wun Tha, U Thiha Saw, and U Pe Myint, and respected Burmese economist U Myint who served as an adviser to President Thein Sein but remains an outspoken, independent-minded, and respected figure who does not appear to have confidence in former or current military leaders.

I also had very candid meetings and interviews with U Khin Aung Myint, speaker of the Upper House, U Shwe Mann, speaker of the Lower House, and two senior ministers attached to the President's Office, U Soe Thane and U Aung Min. I want to thank them for providing me insightful information and granting me interviews during my visits to Burma.

I would also like to thank many of my journalist friends in Thailand. When I spent time at the Foreign Correspondents's Club of Thailand (FCCT) at the Dusit Thani Hotel in Bangkok in the early 1990s, they were the ones who taught me to be independent, to begin my journalistic career, and to search for the truth.

I am deeply grateful to Stephen Bloom, who helped me to clean up my draft manuscript, gave me many thoughtful comments, and helped in correcting and tidying up my English. Without his assistance I could not have completed this book.

My deepest thanks go to Min Zin, Win Thu, Ba Kaung, Kyaw Zwa, Neil Lawrence, Linn Thant, Charles Campbell, and Moe Zaw Oo, who helped to read my final manuscript and offered me helpful suggestions and criticism, as well as intellectual stimulation and personal support. Special thanks to Ba Kaung and Neil Lawrence who helped to compile the endnotes for this book.

I would like to thank my wife Nate who has supported me all the way. Whenever I was depressed or distracted by my work with The Irrawaddy, she gave me the strength to keep writing this book. Along with her, I want to thank my grandmother, who came to Thailand to reunite with me in exile in 2000. She has always been there to help me recharge my batteries whenever they run out.

I am indebted to many of my friends who encouraged me to finish writing this book; Emily Carryer, who edited my manuscript and gave me valuable assistance; and the rest of the staff at Mekong Press in Chiang Mai.

Lastly, I am indebted to Trasvin Jittidecharak of Mekong Press. She and her team gave me a chance to publish this book and provided me with many helpful suggestions. When they first agreed to my initial proposal to write a short piece of just a few thousand words, I did not imagine I would end up writing a book. I want to thank you for your patience and for generously agreeing to publish my first book on Burma.

Chiang Mai
January 2013

1

THE LADY

THE HERO'S DAUGHTER RETURNS

"We want democracy!" my student activist colleagues and I chanted as we marched toward Shwedagon Pagoda in Rangoon. It was August 26, 1988, and we were on our way to hear Aung San Suu Kyi's first public speech, an event that would mark one of the most significant political turning points in the history of Burma. At the time, however, we knew very little of the slim, graceful woman who has since become a pro-democracy icon and who has come to be referred to as "The Lady." We knew that Suu Kyi was the daughter of General Aung San, Burma's beloved military hero who led the struggle for independence from Great Britain, but was assassinated just before that goal was realized. We also knew that she lived abroad and was married to Michael Aris, a British scholar and Tibetologist. We knew little else.

"Can she speak Burmese?" asked one colleague. The answer was yes, but none of us had been sure until two days earlier when Suu Kyi had visited Rangoon General Hospital—the site of a massacre that had occurred on August 10, 1988, when soldiers had opened fire on nurses and activists— and spoke briefly in Burmese to the people gathered outside. We were also unsure of what a woman who had lived comfortably overseas since the age of fifteen would have to say to the suffering people of Burma and young student activists such as me. Regardless of what language she spoke, the real question was whether she could relate to the causes for which we had been fighting: democracy and human rights for the people of Burma. Feeling curious but skeptical as we joined the hundreds of thousands of people gathered outside the pagoda and waited to hear Suu Kyi speak, I reflected on the events that had seasoned me as an activist and brought me to Shwedagon that day.

In 1985, I began to spend time on weekends with a group of intellectuals who were much older than me, most in their fifties and sixties. Some were famous, well-respected poets, writers, editors, publishers, and former political prisoners. These were the people who would later inspire me to become a journalist, and they sparked my interest in Burma's political struggle. Among others, they included Tin Moe, the late poet laureate of Burma, Thaw Ka, Win Tin, and Dagon Taya, a well-respected writer and poet who had been a student activist in the 1930s, as well as a friend of General Aung San.

We began holding regular discussions on Burmese and world literature, and the group became known as the Insein Sarpay Wine, or Insein Literature Circle, because it had been established in Insein Township, the area of Rangoon in which I lived. Many respected literary gurus were invited to address the weekly sessions, and we also met informally throughout the week. In the mornings we would sit in a teashop and share our thoughts on literature or the capital's latest political gossip, then, in the evenings we would go to a liquor store where I saw firsthand how some of Burma's famous writers became heavy drinkers. They did not stop until the last drop had gone.

At first, we carefully avoided sensitive political topics as the gatherings were illegal and we were worried about the possibility of regime agents and informers monitoring our activities. On one occasion a police officer, a writer himself, attended a meeting. His presence panicked some of my colleagues and that day our discussion focused on literature and nothing else.

Despite our attempts otherwise, we soon discovered that it would be impossible to ignore political issues. At one meeting, some former political prisoners who had come back from Coco Island Prison, where they had spent years, raised eyebrows when they brought up the topic of armed struggle. But, despite the fact that the country was stuck in the rut of General Ne Win's "Burmese Way to Socialism," I did not believe that armed struggle was a valid option, because, unlike many militant students at the time, I did not believe it would bring about the desired outcome.

By 1987, everyone was yearning for change in Burma, and although no one knew when it would occur, many were predicting an uprising in the near future. In September, the regime announced the demonetization of all twenty-five, thirty-five, and seventy-five kyat banknotes without compensation, so we attended a small protest, and watched as other students set a government vehicle on fire. The government quickly closed the schools, but not before everyone could see that many students were now ready to go to extreme measures to resist the regime.

As a twenty-year-old botany student at Hlaing Campus (also known as Regional College Two), I became part of an underground student network set up to resist the authoritarian rule of Ne Win's regime, in an effort to help reverse the economic and social hardships it had inflicted on the people of Burma. It was at this time that I also received my first taste of underground publishing. A friend who had been a student activist in the 1970s and was a former political prisoner showed me the antiquated printing cylinder he used to produce underground antigovernment leaflets. This crude device, which worked like a machine rolling out dough, was strictly illegal—anyone found in possession of one was likely to be given a prison sentence of several years. But we were young and idealistic, and believed that students involved in politics should welcome arrest by the oppressive government we were fighting. At the time, being thrown in prison was not only an act of defiance towards the regime, it was also something of an initiation that one had to experience to earn the respect of fellow activists.

My colleagues and I were finally arrested in March 1988, and the harsh reality of what it actually meant to be a political prisoner in Burma was driven home to us one blow at a time.

In the crackdown around the university protests in 1988, my arrest was predictable. In March, a brawl broke out between students and local residents in a teashop near the Rangoon Institute of Technology (RIT). One of those arrested was the son of a local official, and when he was released from police custody, politically active students turned the situation into an antigovernment protest. The government sent in riot police who opened fire on the students. The next day we rushed to the campus, and we saw the blood and heard the stories of the previous night's brutality.

Revolution was in the air and everyone was now looking for an opportunity to rise up and confront the regime. On March 15, 1988, my colleagues and I were sitting in a teashop when we heard that a handful of fellow students were demonstrating and chanting slogans on the RIT campus, so we merged with a group that was marching off to join them.

The riot police had known that we were coming and had blocked the road into the campus. I walked with three other students to speak with the officer in charge, but he was not interested in talking or in letting our group pass to join the other protesters. The officer waved his pistol and several riot police standing behind him aimed their M16 rifles at us. "Do you want me to order them to shoot you now?" he asked. Then, more than twenty military trucks filled with soldiers appeared on the road—a sign that the army had taken over control of the situation from the police. The soldiers looked exhausted, having just been recalled from the front lines of the many ethnic conflicts in the border regions in order to reinforce the troops in Rangoon. Young officers no older than me stared at us as the trucks passed by. One of them pointed at his pistol menacingly.

Realizing how serious the soldiers were about using deadly force to stop us from proceeding, we agreed to retreat to Hlaing Campus. Once back in relative safety, we immediately began to recruit students to join future demonstrations, and on March 17, we staged another protest rally that drew all of the students from the classrooms. We marched around the campus chanting, "Down with the government!" and I joined a group of students who stormed a room where loudspeakers and amplifiers were stored, and after negotiating with a handful of professors, returned to the protest with the equipment.

As the protest continued, a masked student leader gave a speech to hundreds of fellow students, many of whom—including me—also wore masks so as not to be recognized by regime spies. In his fist, the student leader held a letter to be sent to UN Secretary-General Javier Pérez de Cuéllar that contained a list of human rights abuses and the names of students who had been gunned down in protests earlier in the month. Suddenly, riot police stormed the compound and the peaceful protest descended quickly into chaos. I saw the student leader running away as a pursuing officer fired his pistol into the air. I heard another student crying as a policeman grabbed her hair and beat her repeatedly. When a separate group of riot police holding batons closed in, I climbed over the fence like many other students. A female student who could not make it over the top called to me, and I reached back and extended my hand. But I was too late. The police had already captured her.

Those of us who made it to the other side of the fence took refuge in the Inya dormitory where students from the provinces stayed. Soldiers holding automatic machine guns waited outside and circled the compound as the riot police closed in. We all sat tightly, holding hands to resist arrest as blue prison vans began to arrive.

At the moment of our capture we were naively excited. Still carrying our schoolbooks we chanted slogans while we were being transported to Insein Prison in one of the blue vans, alerting people on the streets that we were student protesters being taken to jail. Once inside the infamous prison, which as a young boy I used to pass every day on my way to school, we told the wardens we were hungry and they gave us fried eggs to eat. Then, as night fell, several plainclothes intelligence officers came to observe us, but did not speak. I began to think that the life of an incarcerated political activist was not so bad after all. Others were not so calm. One student who had been seriously injured by riot police during the campus protest crackdown suffered a breakdown and began talking nonstop to the stone-faced officers, who looked clean and educated, and around midnight they snatched the talkative student and took him to be interrogated. After a few hours of beatings he provided details of the student protest movement, returning to the cell a collaborator rather than a colleague. Afterwards, we were each taken for interrogation one by one. When it was my turn, I was taken to an interrogation room in which four intelligence officers were waiting for me. The officer who had escorted me from the cell told the others that I was "one of the guys who was making jokes about us last night." This remark was instantly followed by a punch and a kick, and an order to "kneel down on the floor and be prepared to answer all questions."

"Who are you?" they shouted. "Who were the leaders of the protest?" "Who were the organizers?" "Who gave the speeches?" "Why were you involved?" "Who asked you to join?" Each question was accompanied by another punch and a kick.

Unsatisfied with my answers, the officers ordered me to do one hundred push-ups. I managed only about twenty, which resulted in more physical abuse. Then the officer who was transcribing the affidavit they wanted me to sign, yelled, "You were lying!" tore the paper in half and thundered, "Let's start again. Tell us your name and the names of your parents." Another series of punches left me sprawled out on the floor.

Finally, after two hours the questioning stopped. I crawled back to my cell battered but satisfied because the only true answers I had provided were my own name and the names of my parents. I had not told the interrogators anything about my history as a student activist: about the small underground cell I had formed with my colleagues in 1987 or the antigovernment leaflets we distributed; about the famous elder journalists and writers I was friends with—many of whom were on the government watch list—or the fact that they had inspired my interests in politics and writing; and, of course, I did not tell them that a few months earlier I had received my first taste of publishing in the bedroom of my family home where I had begun to produce samizdat leaflets at night on the old printing cylinder. I also said nothing about what had transpired over the previous week: how, on March 15, I distributed instigating leaflets and joined the march to the RIT; how I organized a protest at Regional College Two; or how I raided the equipment room for loudspeakers so that the student leaders could speak to everyone. What I told the officers in the interrogation room was that on March 17, I came to Rangoon University to meet my friends at a teashop, and when the protest started, we were curious and went to see what was happening, before being mistaken for activists by the riot police who raided the campus.

Back in the cell, I heard the interrogation horror stories of my fellow student prisoners. One had been asked to remove his glasses, and after doing so the intelligence officer asked, "Can you still see me now?" When the student nodded, the officer then punched him in the face. Another student from Kachin State provided his real name, Brang Seng, which also happened to be the name of a Kachin rebel leader. Hearing this, and most likely thinking the student was being defiant, the officer grabbed a wooden stick and hit him repeatedly.

Later in the night, we saw a group of Indian teenagers being brought into the compound. A guard whose eyes were filled with anger informed us that the youths were "looters," then rushed to join the riot police waiting to "welcome" the accused.

Light from the powerful prison spotlight allowed us to watch in horror as riot police and prison guards brutally clubbed each of the boys, killing some. From our cell we shouted at them to stop, but then officials immediately came to our room and blocked the view. The screams and cries continued, and then we heard the sound of gunshots coming from in front of the main prison gate, where authorities had opened fire on people attempting to rescue the van-loads of students and demonstrators still being brought to the prison. The next day, after the drivers of one van evaded local residents attempting to rescue the prisoners they were transporting, the forty-two students and demonstrators crammed inside suffocated to death. We also saw the young Indian men who had been brought to the prison and beaten the night before, at least those who had survived. They were all chained without food or water, and we managed to get them something to drink before they were sent off to forced labor camps in the countryside.

I was fortunate to be released from Insein Prison after one week, but one of my best friends remained behind for several months. Limping from the torture and malnourished because the prison food turned to fish paste and inedible soup after the first night, I rested and recuperated at home for a few weeks, and then began to visit colleagues to map out our future strategy. We decided to expand our network and held several clandestine meetings in Rangoon hideouts in an attempt to evade the watchful eyes of informers and military intelligence. At one secret meeting, a group of students proposed that we engage in armed struggle, arguing that nothing could be accomplished by peaceful means alone. "If you want arms, we can find arms," one student declared. But the rest of us were not prepared to discuss the use of violence. Our preferred methods were to agitate the public, organize labor strikes, and distribute leaflets. In June, we participated in a large, well-planned protest at Rangoon University called the June Affairs. Many more students, including high school students, came to join the protest. This time no troops entered the campus, so we had time to give speeches, and we agreed not to take the protests off-campus. Public sympathy was enormous; many rich people, including some celebrities, either quietly or openly came to offer food, water, and donations.

Eventually, the government closed down the campuses and forced the student protests out into the streets. A deadly government crackdown followed. We saw army trucks drive into crowds of protesters, killing several. My colleague Win Thu joined a group of students who were throwing rocks at a police station, and saw police fire indiscriminately at people around him.

Then, in July, Ne Win resigned as chairman of the ruling Burma Socialist Programme Party (BSPP). If his resignation was intended to calm the restless country, however, he accomplished just the opposite by provocatively saying in his resignation speech, "I want the entire nation, the people, to know that if in the future there are more disturbances, if the army shoots it will shoot to hit; there will be no firing into the sky to scare."

Hundreds of people were gunned down over the following month, and protesters soon realized that Ne Win was being true to his word. Faced with a choice between going underground and continuing to openly protest, which would carry a high risk of either being sent back to Insein Prison or being killed, my activist friends and I decided to go into hiding in Rangoon. After a friendly local official told me that intelligence officers had shown him my photo and asked my whereabouts, I quickly left the city and fled to the home of close relatives in Kayan. My mother followed a few days later and upon her arrival I could instantly see she was nervous and afraid. "They came and looked for you last night at our house," she whispered.

By chance, a respected abbot from Day Pauk village was visiting my relatives' house when my mother informed me about the unwanted visitors. When the monk heard that military intelligence officers were after me, he immediately offered me accommodation at his monastery, the well-known Day Pauk Kyaung. I gratefully accepted, and within the hour was aboard a boat with the abbot, heading along a small creek to the monastery. As we passed people on the shore or in other boats, they all paid their respects to this revered monk.

Day Pauk Kyaung was a rundown temple and housed only a few monks, but it sat in a beautiful location between rice paddies a few kilometers from Day Pauk village. The morning after my arrival the abbot shaved my head—I could not say no—and the poor children living in the temple danced around, welcoming me as a new friend to their remote monastery. We ate the alms the monks collected that morning and then the abbot gave me a set of robes.

"You are now *koyin gyi* [a novice monk]," he said with a broad smile. "Don't worry, I will protect you. Just don't say who you are and where you come from."

The abbot gave me a mantra to chant every morning to keep danger at bay and avoid capture by military intelligence. Although he kept most of his thoughts to himself, he was clearly political. When news of the bloody suppression of the student protests in August reached the monastery, the abbot openly told an assembly of local villagers that they had to fight for justice.

My mother visited once again and told me that some of my former student comrades were also in hiding in upper Burma, and that a number of them were also in monasteries. Others had been caught and were in prison where they were being tortured. She also told me that student activists were still holding small, sporadic protests in Rangoon. Cut off from all of this I felt lonely and restless at the monastery. Meditation did not help. I yearned for news from Rangoon and elsewhere in the country, and rejoiced when a local farmer brought an old radio to the temple, which, after being repaired by one of the monks, allowed me to hear broadcasts by the Burmese Service of the BBC. There were very few radios in Day Pauk, and most villagers wanting to hear news of outside events gathered at the house of the village headman to listen to his. In the candlelit corners of his home they sat and smoked their cheroots while reports came in of the bloodshed in Rangoon. I joined them once when my radio needed repair, and while the villagers greeted me with respect the village headman seemed suspicious.

I already suspected that the headman and villagers had seen through my disguise because at one religious ceremony attended by monks and abbots from other monasteries I was unable to join in the chants as they were all in the Pali language. The local people in attendance stared at me and began to whisper and laugh. I was also sure that the owner of my old radio who visited me most evenings and puffed away on his long cheroot wondered why a young monk was so interested in listening to BBC broadcasts and never talked about monastic life, but he never asked.

The abbot seemed unconcerned about the possibility that I might be exposed as a bogus monk. As evidence, the day after my faux pas at the ceremony, a woman and her young daughter came to the monastery and handed me a meat dish, something they never would have done without the abbot's approval. The abbot also followed the news from Rangoon very closely and often engaged in heated political debates with other monks. When he was absent, I sometimes joined an assistant monk on boat trips to other villages. We often arrived just as families were settling down for their evening meal, and, while unable to partake himself because of his monastic vows, my companion asked them to prepare some tasty dishes for his hungry young activist friend.

On August 8, 1988, students called for the nationwide protest that became known as the 8888 uprising. I soon heard news of more violence in Rangoon: eyewitnesses confirmed that troops had opened fire indiscriminately on peaceful demonstrators and onlookers, and into houses and shops. I desperately wanted to return, but all roads leading to the city were blocked. The killings came to a halt after five days on August 13, when new president Sein Lwin resigned. Afterwards, the army withdrew from the public eye and Dr. Maung Maung, a historian and Ne Win's protégé, became president. This was not enough to stem the swell of rebellion, however, and the general strike continued as people wanted once and for all to see the end of the brutal repression and the BSPP that exercised it.

Eventually it became safe enough for me to leave the monastery. But before I left, and still in monk's robes, I addressed the students and villagers at a mass protest that had been organized by a school principal and a teacher. When I confessed that I was not a real monk, the owner of the old radio that had kept me so well informed smiled and applauded, saying he had known of my disguise all along.

By the time I returned to Rangoon in late August the uprising was in full swing. I soon reunited with friends who had recently been released from prisons and interrogation centers. Others, like me, had been hiding in temples disguised as monks, and when Aung San Suu Kyi stepped in front of the crowd at Shwedagon Pagoda on August 26 to make her first public speech, our hair had barely grown to stubble length.

Aung San Suu Kyi was the child of a happy union. Her father, Aung San, who was assassinated by a political rival in 1947 when she was just two, fell deeply in love with Khin Kyi, a beautiful senior staff nurse who treated him for injuries he suffered during a World War II campaign, and they married in 1942. Aung San is an iconic figure in Burma, and although it is many years since he was murdered he has remained a prominent figure in Burmese politics. Many students who joined the peaceful protests in 1988 held Aung San's portrait, and one slogan we repeatedly shouted was, "Aung San did not train the military to kill its own people!"

Despite the fact that Suu Kyi is the daughter of a man who was a military and political legend, some of her close friends believe that it was, in fact, her mother who was her true political and cultural mentor, and the inspiration behind her rise to prominence.[1] While Khin Kyi never shared the fame of her husband and daughter, she was successful in her own right, and while she was alive was regarded as one of Burma's most influential women. She was a member of Burma's parliament from 1947 until 1952, became chairperson of the Women's Association of Burma in the 1950s, and was a leading light in other social organizations. In 1960, she became Burma's first and only female ambassador, representing her country in India and also taking special responsibility for Nepal. Khin Kyi's achievements were rewarded abroad with honors from the United States, Yugoslavia, and Thailand, and at home the Burmese government presented her with the Maha Thiri Thudhamma Prize given for services to Burmese social and religious life.

In the midst of the 1988 uprising, Suu Kyi, who had lived abroad since the age of fifteen, returned to her homeland to care for Khin Kyi, who had become terminally ill. Looking back, it appeared that fate and circumstance conspired both to bring Suu Kyi back to Burma just when the country needed her, and to allow her to begin her political career at the right place and the right time.

Once she had returned to Rangoon, Suu Kyi began to receive news of the unrest and the killing of student protesters. She then spoke to Ohn Myint, a revered member of the independence movement and friend of her father's, and asked to meet with Ne Win. Ne Win refused to meet her and sent a message back saying, "We understood you were not going to get involved in politics."[2] Rumors were circling that Ne Win would soon resign, so Ohn Myint felt that Suu Kyi should not alert him that she was interested in entering the political fray in such a volatile situation. Nevertheless, she replied to Ne Win, "I meant if I lived overseas I would not be involved in politics." Suu Kyi believed that making Ne Win aware of her intentions clarified that she was not interested in an underground movement and armed resistance; she preferred to practice politics within the rule of law, sticking to Gandhi's principle of nonviolent struggle.

After the killings on August 8, 1988, Suu Kyi prepared to send a letter of appeal to President Sein Lwin who had assumed the office of head of state after Ne Win had stepped aside, but he also suddenly resigned.

Then, on August 13, while Suu Kyi and Ohn Myint sat in the living room of her lakeside house planning their next move, news arrived that the mass murders in Burma had stopped.

After hearing this news, Suu Kyi met with then commander-in-chief Dr. Maung Maung, Khin Kyi's family lawyer and personal friend. She informed him that she was entering politics and wanted to seek his advice to help solve the ongoing conflict. Maung Maung took Suu Kyi into the prayer room to talk to her in private. The former judge explained the risks of entering politics and kindly warned her that she would probably suffer as a result. He also told her that because he was now in the government it would be difficult to meet casually with her. Suu Kyi listened attentively and they parted amicably, but nothing was resolved and they had no chance to meet again.

Suu Kyi remained undaunted, however, and on August 24, 1988, when she visited Rangoon General Hospital to commemorate the victims of the massacre on August 10, a group of her friends, including Ohn Myint, writer Maung Thaw Ka, and film director Moe Thu, persuaded her to speak to the public.[3] She spoke briefly that day, telling the people to be disciplined, and then sent a letter to government leaders offering to become a mediator between the students and the government.

Before her first public speech at Shwedagon Pagoda, Suu Kyi sent her husband a letter entitled, "The Reason to Enter Politics," in which she said she had been devastated to see the deterioration of her country, and had decided to stay in Burma to work towards achieving a political system that would benefit its citizens. Although she wanted to avoid power politics and conflict, she felt that she had to become involved out of gratitude to her father.

As we listened to Suu Kyi speak on that hot August morning in 1988, it became clear that she was determined to formally become a leader of the uprising, and that nothing could make her leave her native Burma. Suu Kyi articulately delivered her speech in Burmese, speaking in the same straightforward style that her father was known to have done. She said, "I believe that all the people who have assembled here have without exception come with the unshakable desire to strive for and win a multiparty democratic system. . . . In order to arrive at this objective, all the people should march united in a disciplined manner towards the goal of democracy."[4] The sincerity in her voice and the power of her message hooked the crowd immediately, and she went on to address the concerns that my colleagues and I had discussed on the way to the rally. "I would like to explain the part I have played in this movement," she said. "This is needed because a fair number of people are not very well acquainted with my personal history. It is only natural and right that those who do not know me would like to know some facts."

Suu Kyi acknowledged that because she had spent most of her life abroad and was married to a foreigner, many were skeptical about whether she was familiar enough with Burmese politics and the issues facing the people. However, she said her time abroad and her marriage had never interfered with, or lessened, her love for and devotion to Burma. She pointed out that her family understood as well as anyone how complicated and dangerous Burmese politics could be, and that a leader must be willing to suffer the ultimate sacrifice on this account, as her father had done.

As her speech gained momentum, everyone began to accept that although Suu Kyi had been abroad for most of her adult life, her family history—together with her knowledge, intellect, and passion for her country—instantly qualified her to assume a leadership mantle in Burma's second independence movement.

At that moment, my colleagues and I realized that this petite woman would soon became an enormous thorn in the side of the powerful military, because she had the integrity, steadfastness of purpose, and ability to command the loyalty of the people—traits the generals loathed. Our private predictions were ultimately realized as Suu Kyi's speech at Shwedagon was, in fact, the start of a long political journey that would lead to endless confrontation with the generals, futile calls for political dialogue, the regime's outright denial of her role in Burmese politics, and long periods of house arrest. Suu Kyi may have arrived at Shwedagon Pagoda that day as not much more than a curiosity, but she left as the leader of a newly invigorated opposition movement that took to the streets once again in protest.

TWO LOST DECADES

Aung Sang Suu Kyi's speech at Shwedagon Pagoda in August 1988 filled us with hope that the plight of Burma's people would soon be over. It was not to be. The speech marked the start of two decades of dashed hopes and disappointment for Suu Kyi and the democracy movement inside Burma, with Suu Kyi spending fifteen of the next twenty-two years under house arrest.

On September 12, 1988, less than a month after Suu Kyi declared her entry into politics, a US naval fleet of five warships, including the aircraft carrier Coral Sea, was spotted in Burmese territorial waters. The US embassy said the fleet had been sent for the evacuation of embassy staff, but rumors spread throughout Burma that the United States was preparing to launch an invasion. Activists who believed the rumors even began distributing leaflets claiming the marines were on their way. But rather than US marines coming to assist the demonstrators, Burmese soldiers came to mow them down. Less than a week later, and seemingly undeterred by this international attention, the military launched a deadly crackdown on demonstrators that had been planned in advance by General Saw Maung and his fellow coup leaders at the Defense Ministry. The September 18 massacre was systematic and cold-blooded murder, as troops came with machine guns and automatic rifles, storming a protest center where demonstrators were staging hunger strikes and sit-in protests. Even a group of demonstrators who held a peaceful protest in front of the US embassy, where they felt they would be protected, were slaughtered in a mass killing that was caught on camera. Some gunshot victims who were still alive were believed to have been secretly cremated, while the luckier ones were taken to hospital emergency wards with missing limbs and chest wounds. It seemed the regime did not care who saw this brutality.

In the late afternoon on the day of the massacre, my colleagues and I walked into the criminal investigation department of the police headquarters on Lower Mingaladon Road in Insein. Several police officers that had previously joined the protests welcomed us, but they looked uncomfortable in front of other senior officers. To everyone's surprise, one of my colleagues suddenly asked them whether they could give us basic military training. While this drew uncomfortable laughter and chuckles from several of the policemen, one grabbed my friend's shoulder and berated him. "Are you crazy?" the officer asked. "You can't ask that kind of question in front of everyone. Come back later."

We withdrew to a teashop, and as we discussed our next move several military trucks drove in to clear the streets of Insein that had been in chaos since that morning when soldiers had shot several demonstrators protesting in the area. Using loudspeakers, the soldiers announced that the armed forces had taken power and that everyone must return home before 6:00 p.m. A military coup had taken place: the BSPP had been removed from power and martial law had been declared. As soon as the announcement had been made, a man sitting next to us shot at the soldiers with a *jingalee*, a slingshot. In a split second, soldiers returned fire and we all hit the floor as the brave *jingalee*-wielding man fled. Although the soldiers were well armed, they did not dare chase him though Rangoon's narrow backstreets.

Once the soldiers had left we retreated to a local restaurant, where the sympathetic owner told us that everyone could stay overnight. However, several of the protest leaders were concerned for all of our security as they anticipated that the military would come and raid the restaurant soon. They told us to leave, so we moved on.

The following day, my colleagues and I quietly went back to the police headquarters where two officers showed us how to dismantle and fire a machine gun and rifles that looked older than me and had no bullets. "*Jingalees* are better," my friend quipped. A few hours later, police officers informed us that the army would soon take over the headquarters, so all visitors had to evacuate.

During the following week, the military generals who had staged the coup formed the State Law and Order Restoration Council (SLORC), which became the new ruling junta. Then, on September 25, 1988, Suu Kyi met with the highly regarded journalist Win Tin and asked him to join her new political party, the National League for Democracy (NLD). Win Tin hesitated at first, wanting time to consider. But an impatient Suu Kyi pushed him for a quick response. "Do not postpone," she said. "I am forming the party in two days."[5] Win Tin then agreed to become a member, along with Aung Gyi and Tin Oo who had both been close colleagues of Ne Win. With the trio of Suu Kyi, Aung Gyi, and Tin Oo comprising a formidable party base, many other politicians, intellectuals, and military veterans flocked to join the NLD soon after its formation on September 27, 1988.

At around the same time that the NLD was formed, I decided to leave Rangoon and head to the Thai border where young people like me were taking up arms against the Burmese military. Before departing I went back to see my mother, who had always supported my younger brother and me in our political activity and taught us not to be afraid of anything. She readily permitted me to leave home for Thailand, and on the day I left she offered me a few thousand kyat. Kneeling down, I paid respect to her and my grandmother, whose eyes expressed concern but who never interfered with my mother's decision not to prevent me from leaving. "Keep on fighting," my mother said. "You will come back soon and we will meet again."

After leaving Rangoon, I traveled to Three Pagodas Pass where I was reunited with my friend and colleague, Win Thu. The journey there was dangerous. Escorted by Mon rebels carrying AK47 rifles, we walked for two weeks, largely at night, through jungle and contested military zones. Initially, ten of us stayed in a temporary hut in the jungle. We all suffered from malaria, and after a few months only three of us were left in the camp: the rest had gone back when the new junta announced that students could return and promised they would not be punished. Despite the regime's promises, however, some of my colleagues were arrested when they tried to go back to Rangoon. One jumped out of a train while handcuffed and escaped, but intelligence officers caught him again in one of the campus protests and sentenced him to ten years in prison. In addition to being harassed by the new military regime, many others who went back suffered from depression and struggled to return to normal life.

As for me, although I lived briefly in the jungle where a Mon ethnic rebel group had their headquarters, I chose not to join an armed resistance group. I decided that my contribution to the dissident movement would be to use my passion for politics and journalism to educate the international community about what was happening inside Burma. I crossed the border into Thailand and traveled by bus to Bangkok, always watchful of regular identity-card inspections carried out by Thai immigration officials. Two years later, I founded the Burma Information Group (BIG), with the mission of documenting human rights violations in Burma, particularly the unlawful detention of members of the pro-democracy opposition and other dissident and ethnic groups. BIG was an independent information group and was not affiliated with any political organization. It released several reports on the internal situation in Burma, and provided news and information to Amnesty International, Human Rights Watch Asia, and other human rights agencies, as well as to Bangkok-based newspapers such as *The Nation* and the *Bangkok Post*.

While I was getting my journalistic feet wet in Bangkok, Suu Kyi was gaining popularity among ordinary people in Burma, although not with the generals. On one famous occasion during a visit to the Irrawaddy Delta in August 1989, she confronted soldiers who aimed their rifles at her. The same year, the SLORC had decided to hold a national election, purportedly to form a new civilian government. During the run-up to the election, Suu Kyi's popularity scared the junta to such an extent that they placed her under house arrest. Despite her detention, the NLD shocked the military regime and the world by winning the 1990 general election by a landslide, taking around 80 percent of the seats contested in polling that was free and fair.

With the people of Burma punishing the regime at the polls, I began contemplating a return home. My mother sent me a letter through a diplomatic channel full of optimism and joy that her predicted reunion of two years earlier would soon come true. "My son, you are coming back soon!" she wrote. "We all celebrated the victory here. We all went out and voted for the NLD. . . . Even the soldiers voted for the NLD. People here said that all students in exile must return home. So I hope to see you in a few months. We are all going to be reunited soon." My mother's joy, however, did not last long. She soon realized, like everyone else, that the regime had no plans to hand over power.

The author as a young journalist, Bangkok, 1992. Courtesy Nic Dunlop

Suu Kyi had seen this coming long beforehand. Nineteen days prior to being placed under house arrest, she had told a correspondent from *Asiaweek*, "Day by day we are losing more of our basic political rights,"[6] adding that the NLD had complained to the SLORC about the lack of special provisions for the transfer of power after the election, but the SLORC had ignored the party's protests. When asked how power would be transferred to the new government after the election, she simply replied, "We don't know, this is the problem," continuing that unless the transfer provisions were known, the people could not trust the SLORC to set up a democratically elected government.

She was later proved correct. The junta launched a major crackdown during which it arrested approximately three hundred NLD members, including most senior leaders, and effectively decapitated the organization. The junta then nullified the results of the election, and not only would my mother and I not be reunited soon, we would never meet again.

My mother died in August 1994 when a reckless truck driver hit her while she was riding on a trishaw, killing her instantly. I received the devastating news in Bangkok, where I was running my magazine *The Irrawaddy* in its infant stages and writing regular articles and op-ed pieces that were critical of the regime in *The Nation* and *Bangkok Post* newspapers. Neither my brother nor I could attend our mother's funeral. At the time she died, my brother was serving a ten-year sentence in Insein Prison for taking part in a protest commemorating Suu Kyi's Nobel Peace Prize in December 1991. When he was arrested, the regime accused him of also having connections with underground communists. Junta authorities refused my brother's request to attend our mother's funeral, and I was also unable to return from exile because intelligence officers were always monitoring our "rebel house," which even my friends were afraid to visit for fear of showing up on the junta's radar screen. The best I could do to honor my mother was to have a foreign diplomat friend lay a wreath on my behalf. However, I did manage to establish the first phone conversation in many years with my colleagues and my grandmother, and every one of them repeated the same refrain: "Don't come back!" Later, intelligence officers came to see my grandmother and asked her to write a letter calling me home to Burma. She refused, and asked them to leave her home.

At this time, Suu Kyi was virtually trapped inside Rangoon and, despite being released from house arrest in 1995, the following decade was fraught with frustrated attempts to leave the city. By 1995, the country had fallen under the control of an emerging dictator, Senior General Than Shwe, with no path to democracy in sight. To prevent Suu Kyi from regenerating the passions among the populace that had led to the 1988 uprising, the junta consistently tried to prevent her from leaving Rangoon, and when she did get out, they harassed her. Soon after her release, Suu Kyi made a trip to Karen State to meet with Thamanya Sayadaw, a highly revered monk. Analysts saw this trip not only as a religious pilgrimage, but also as a test of the terms of Suu Kyi's "unconditional release." Despite being followed by intelligence officers she returned safely. The Lady continued to press the regime, however, and the more the military leaders suppressed her efforts to leave, the stronger her status grew.

Suu Kyi and other NLD members were forced to cancel a March 1996 trip to Mandalay to attend a supporters' trial after the train they were booked

Tin Oo (*top, second from left*), Suu Kyi, and Kyi Maung (*top, second from right*) give speeches over the gate of Suu Kyi's University Avenue house in 1996. Courtesy Nic Dunlop

on developed a suspicious last-minute problem. Then, in November of that year, about two hundred members of the junta-backed Union Solidarity and Development Association (USDA)—a civilian organization created by the junta in 1993 that the generals used in whatever manner necessary to advance their cause among the general population—attacked her car, hitting it with iron bars and smashing the rear window, while nearby troops and police watched but did not intervene.

In August 1998, Suu Kyi left her home to meet NLD members outside Rangoon. As in previous attempts, authorities blocked her en route. After a thirteen-day standoff on a bridge outside Rangoon, she succumbed to illness and dehydration and was forced to turn back. In early September 1999, she made a trip to Dala, Rangoon Division, where two hundred riot police surrounded her motorcade, and after a nine-day standoff forced them to return to Rangoon.

Being confined to Rangoon was not only designed to hamper Suu Kyi's political influence, it was also designed to weaken her individually. In 1999,

Suu Kyi's husband Michael Aris died of prostate cancer at the age of fifty-three, after having been repeatedly denied visas to see his wife for the three years leading up to his death. The regime said it would allow Suu Kyi to fly out of the country to meet her dying husband, but she was certain they would not allow her back into Burma.[7] Ultimately, Suu Kyi and Aris decided together that she must remain in the country to fight for Burma's freedom.

Suu Kyi was again prevented from leaving Rangoon in September 2000, when security forces stopped her from boarding a train for Mandalay, the country's second largest city, and arrested dozens of her supporters at the capital's main railway station. This time, she was forcibly taken back to her home and placed under house arrest for the second time.

In October, high-ranking intelligence unit officials from the regime came to meet Suu Kyi at her house, and Malaysian diplomat Razali Ismail, the UN-appointed envoy to Burma, later confirmed the news that a "secret dialogue" was taking place.[8] These clandestine discussions were backed by the UN, United States, the EU, Japan, and the Association of Southeast Asian Nations (ASEAN), and everyone was optimistic about their success. As hoped, the regime began to release a small number of political prisoners, including NLD members, and rumors surfaced that Suu Kyi had agreed to abandon the 1990 election results and would join an emergency committee alongside the generals. None of the rumors turned out to be true, however, and it was not until May 6, 2002, that Suu Kyi was released, after spending nineteen months under house arrest.

In the months following Suu Kyi's release there were no political breakthroughs, and in reference to the supposedly continuing "secret dialogue" between Suu Kyi and the junta, U Lwin, the secretary of the NLD, told reporters who questioned what was stalling the discussion, that "it has not stalled because it hasn't even started yet."[9] It was unclear whether the generals were changing tactics to counter Suu Kyi, or simply ignoring her in an effort to frustrate her and provoke her into a confrontation that would provide them with an excuse to crack down on her and her supporters once again. She was, in fact, frustrated, not only with the regime but also with her supporters in Rangoon. After her second release, Suu Kyi confided to her aides that she was disappointed to see that people in the capital had become apolitical. As a result, she wanted to go to the countryside, where she hoped to meet more politically active people.[10] So, in early 2003, she decided to test her boundaries, and traveled to Shan State, Arakan State, Chin State, Kachin State, Sagaing Division, and Mandalay. Wherever she went, tens of thousands of people welcomed her, and the opposition movement once again gained political momentum. Suu Kyi, Tin Oo, and the other NLD members who accompanied them from Rangoon were surprised to see the overwhelming and spontaneous support they received. It seemed, at first, that Suu Kyi had been right to get out of "Big Brother's" capital of Rangoon.

The generals were well aware of Suu Kyi's countrywide travels, and thugs and USDA members regularly followed her convoy and harassed the rallies. In May 2003, during her trip to Myitkyina, Kachin State, people armed with catapults and small objects such as bicycle nuts tried to keep Suu Kyi's vehicle from crossing a bridge into the town. "They were just showing their force, and our people suggested that they open the road,"[11] said U Lwin. "Finally they moved away." He called the standoff, "the most serious incident" of Aung San Suu Kyi's trip thus far. No injuries were reported, but these incidents soon escalated.

On May 30, Suu Kyi's driver sensed something was wrong as the motorcade arrived after dark into a remote area in central Burma near Depayin. Although supporters from Sagaing and Monywa were following Suu Kyi's convoy on motorcycles, police roadblocks prevented most of them from accompanying her motorcade into Depayin. Then, two elderly monks stopped the motorcade and asked Suu Kyi to make a speech.[12] Suspecting the monks could be imposters, Suu Kyi's driver and bodyguards wanted to drive on. Before they could do so, however, four or five busloads of USDA members and thugs armed with bamboo sticks, iron bars, and knives swarmed Suu Kyi's convoy, jumped on the cars, and attacked them in a ruthless and systematic fashion. One witness described, "The attackers beat women and pulled off their longyi [skirts] and their blouses. When victims, covered in blood, fell to the ground, the attackers grabbed their hair and pounded their heads on the pavement until their bodies stopped moving. The whole time, the attackers were screaming the words, 'Die, die, die . . .' There was so much blood. I still cannot get rid of the sight of people, covered in blood, being beaten mercilessly to death."[13]

Tin Oo was dragged from the car, severely beaten, and then arrested. In 2010, he told journalists that he witnessed several groups of about fifty people moving in to attack the convoy. The thugs, he said, were trained and well prepared. Suu Kyi told her driver she could not leave her people and asked him to stop the car, and when the mob attacked she did not order him to drive away, as her bodyguards outside the car fought back. Finally, however, he decided to save her himself and sped off. They escaped the attack, but as soon as they arrived at Yae-U, security officers were waiting and arrested them. Suu Kyi's driver was locked up and tortured by authorities, who seemed angry that he had rescued Suu Kyi.

It is estimated that about eighty people were killed at Depayin, but no one knows how many for certain. Dissident sources placed the number in the hundreds, while the regime reported that only four people were killed and fifty injured. As the regime planned, there were no cameras or journalists to officially record the nighttime carnage. There was no doubt that the regime was behind the well-organized attack, but it was not known whether they wanted to kill Suu Kyi or just intimidate her. After Depayin, the regime announced that both Suu Kyi and Tin Oo were being kept in protective custody. In addition, all senior NLD officers were placed under house arrest, party offices were shut down, and the party's phone lines were cut.

It was found out via a tip-off to the BBC by British Foreign Officer Mike O'Brien that Suu Kyi was being held in Insein Prison, and after intensive negotiations with the regime's leaders, UN special envoy Razali Ismail was allowed to meet with her for thirty minutes. Upon meeting Ismail inside the prison, Suu Kyi's first words were, "I want justice, Raz."

In March 2004, Suu Kyi met Razali Ismail again, this time after her transfer back to house arrest. This was the last time they met. She reiterated her readiness to meet the generals, despite the events at Depayin, for the sake of the people. "Suu Kyi had come a long way to realize that democracy can only be done through the generals, with the latter still in the driving seat,"

Razali wrote. "This realization of hers is in stark contrast to the imperious, principled, and unbending Suu Kyi I had met over twenty meetings ago. She was hugely concerned as to how far behind Myanmar [Burma] was compared to its neighbors." However, the UN envoy said that he was unable to make the generals recognize and acknowledge the changes in Suu Kyi. Than Shwe continued to label her a marionette of the West, and pursued efforts to make Suu Kyi irrelevant to Burma.

Five years later, in 2009, Suu Kyi was finally due to be released from house arrest yet again. But in May, about two weeks before she was set to gain her freedom, a man from Missouri named John Yettaw reportedly strapped on homemade flippers and illegally swam across the lake to her home. The fifty-three-year-old Mormon, who said he had been sent by God to deliver a warning that Suu Kyi would be assassinated, stayed uninvited in Suu Kyi's home for two nights.[14] Yettaw received a seven-year sentence, but on August 15, 2009, the regime agreed to deport him. It is still a mystery whether Yettaw actually swam to Suu Kyi's house or whether it was a junta setup to extend her detention; there are numerous conspiracy theories about who may have helped him, how they did so, and what their motives were. But because she sheltered him in her home, Suu Kyi was sentenced to an additional eighteen months under house arrest, conveniently long enough to prevent her from taking part in the 2010 election. Suu Kyi's lawyer called Yettaw "a fool," and said her supporters were "very angry with this wretched American."[15]

All in all, by 2010, Suu Kyi had spent fifteen of the twenty-two years since her speech at Shwedagon locked inside her University Avenue residence. During that time, I followed her struggle from Thailand and watched as the horrifying and depressing scene unfolded inside my country.

For obvious reasons, the regime did not like me, or my publication. The journalistic activities in which I was engaged as an exile would have put me in prison for years inside Burma. Brigadier General Khin Nyunt, then the junta's intelligence chief, once asked a visiting Thai army chief, General Chetta Thanajaro, if he could help stop my regular columns from appearing in The Nation. The Thai general's staff referred my case to the Thai Foreign Ministry, who called my editor at The Nation. The editor informed me about the meeting in Rangoon, told me that Khin Nyunt had personally mentioned my name, and said that he could not provide me with any protection. He kindly requested that I "lay low for a few months."

A short time later, Burma's intelligence service arrested Ye Htut, my colleague in Rangoon, and sentenced him to seven years in prison for sending me "concocted and false information." When reporting on the story, The New Light of Myanmar, a state-run newspaper, published two photos: one of Ye Htut and one of another man that was said to be me, but, in fact, was someone else. Afterwards, when a Burmese opposition member living in exile called and told me that a senior Thai intelligence officer wanted to see me, I went into hiding. My colleague later called again and said that Thai officials had told him that I had been sent back to Burma via the border crossing at Mae Sot. I assumed that whoever was actually sent back to Burma was either a different person named Aung Zaw, or the man in the newspaper photo.

Major Aung Lynn Htut, a defector from the Burmese military who served in the counter intelligence unit, told me in 2008 that he and his colleagues followed Ye Htut and me. He said, "We opened his letters, read them, and then resealed them and sent them to your address in Bangkok." Ye Htut had no idea this was taking place. He regularly went to the general post office in Rangoon and sent letters to me in Bangkok, until he was arrested. His letters, while full of grievances and skepticism about the regime, contained no statistics, figures, or political analysis, and never advocated subversive action. Like everyone else, after the generals nullified the NLD's landslide victory, Ye Htut felt he had been robbed and was doubtful that the generals would give up their hold on power. His letters were simply the reflections of an ordinary Burmese citizen observing daily life in Rangoon. For this "crime," he served his full seven-year sentence in prison.

In 1995, The Irrawaddy relocated its office to Chiang Mai, northern Thailand, less than 400 kilometers from Rangoon. Then, in 2000, I was reunited with my younger brother, who had spent eight years in prison, and my grandmother. The same year, The Irrawaddy launched an online news service providing daily news coverage on Burma; the online version is now regarded as one of the most credible news services on the country. Although

Monks protest during the 2007 Saffron Revolution.

the website, along with Reuters, BBC, Voice of America (VOA), *Bangkok Post*, Democratic Voice of Burma (DVB), and YouTube, was officially blocked inside Burma until September 2011, many of the younger generation found ways to gain access and feed our news organization information about what was happening within the country. This became especially important during the 2007 Saffron Revolution when both professional and amateur journalists risked all to provide information to the outside world on the junta's ruthless suppression of monk- and student-led protests.

The Saffron Revolution was instigated on August 15, 2007, when the regime decided to increase fuel prices by 500 percent. Students and opposition activists launched protests, and on September 5, the junta forcefully broke up a peaceful demonstration by monks in Pakokku, Magwe Division. The sangha, Burma's community of monks, demanded an apology by September 17, and when that did not arrive they began to lead marches and protests joined by thousands of people. The junta, using both the military and USDA thugs, attempted to suppress the protesters and break up the marches.[16] When the demonstrations continued, the junta ordered a state of emergency, imposed a curfew, banned gatherings of more than five people, and declared certain monasteries off limits. Then, on September 26, its security forces cracked down on the protesters using bullets, teargas, and batons. Thousands were arrested and taken to detention centers, and dozens of monasteries were raided, looted, and ransacked.

The international community was outraged, and the United States, EU, Canada, and Australia tightened economic sanctions against top Burmese officials. The UN Security Council issued a statement condemning the crackdown, and the UN Human Rights Council passed a resolution "strongly deploring" the violent crackdown on the peaceful protests.[17] But the condemnations of the international community fell largely on the deaf ears of the generals. House-to-house raids and arrests continued for the next couple of months, with family members of some protesters being detained as hostages for the return of their outlaw kin.

The next year, the regime announced that it would hold a national referendum on its controversial draft constitution, which had been written by the generals and approved by a sham national constitutional convention. The referendum was held in the immediate aftermath of the tragic Cyclone Nargis in 2008, which devastated large parts of the south of the country and left at least 138,000 dead and many more homeless. After the referendum, the junta announced that an impossible 98 percent of the population had voted, and that 92 percent had approved the new constitution.

In early 2010, the regime called for a general election before the end of the year. Unsurprisingly in a Junta-initiated election, the 2010 election process within Burma was far from fair. Six months before the election, in May 2010, the junta published details of its newly proclaimed Political Parties Registration Law, which required all existing political parties to re-register by May 7, 2010, or face dissolution, and banned anyone serving a prison term from founding, or being a member of, a political party. These laws excluded more than two thousand political prisoners, including Aung San Suu Kyi, from politics. The laws also meant that the NLD had to re-register without naming Suu Kyi and the other party leaders still detained by the regime as members, or face the prospect of being officially disbanded by the regime.

Whether or not to re-register provided the NLD with a major dilemma, and a crack soon appeared in the party. One camp, led by Chairman Aung Shwe, favored re-registration, another camp, led by Win Tin and supported by the NLD youth wing, opposed re-registration on the grounds that the election laws were unfair and undemocratic. As the NLD leadership debated the issue in Rangoon, a grass-roots movement in opposition to re-registration began to take hold in the countryside, and several of its leaders openly told exile media that they favored a boycott of the election. If the party decided to re-register, they argued, it would lose its integrity.

Suu Kyi then entered the fray, issuing a statement through her lawyer that she would not think of having the NLD re-register under the unjust election law. "She wanted party members to know that the party would have no dignity if it registers and participates in the election,"[18] he said. However, Suu Kyi did not order the NLD to follow her lead, saying that "neither she nor anyone else owns the party."[19] This left party members to make the decision themselves, democratically, through a vote which was held on March 29, 2010 with around 160 NLD representatives from across Burma. Aung Shwe and other leaders who favored re-registration did not participate. But while the ninety-two-year-old party chairman did not participate in the meeting, a party spokesperson said he sent a letter stating that he would follow Suu Kyi's decision.[20] "She is our leader," Aung Shwe reportedly told his aides.

The decision not to re-register was predictable, but the consequences were not and the decision was therefore controversial. Some analysts said that instead of taking the moral high ground, the NLD should have re-registered without Suu Kyi and the other incarcerated leaders and exposed the injustices of the election laws to the people of Burma and the international community. Critics said the NLD's decision not to take part in the election was a hastily made, self-defeating political blunder, and missed an opportunity that played into the hands of the regime.

In Burma, however, many people welcomed the NLD decision, saying the party would no longer be a respectable organization if it decided to

A young woman casts her vote.

register under the regime's unjust election laws. And in her statement, Suu Kyi said that the party would not come to an end regardless of whether or not it decided to re-register. She said that that she would continue her efforts to bring democracy to Burma and told her lawyers that if the imprisoned former student leader Min Ko Naing of the 88 Generation Students group could fight for democracy in Burma without a political signpost, she could do the same.

The regime held Burma's first election since the 1990 nullified NLD landslide, a week prior to the release of Suu Kyi. This time, the generals left nothing to chance, manipulating the outcome so that their newly-formed USDP, staffed by recently-resigned military top brass, walked away with more than 75 percent of the seats contested. Many at the time labeled the November election a charade: a deadly serious, long-running game meant to keep senior military officials in power for decades to come.

It was hard to read the generals' minds and political motives. However, the election seemed to legitimize Burma's ruling class. They realized that they could not continue as a reviled military dictatorship, and decided that it was better to stay in power while making a minor concession to merely shed their green uniforms. The then US Assistant Secretary of State for Public Affairs P. J. Crowley commented when asked to share the United States, reaction to the retired generals' participation under the civilian banner, "It's more about what they do on behalf of their country and whether, in becoming civilians, they are willing to serve the interests of the entire society, in this case, Burma, as opposed to the narrow constituency of and narrow interest of the junta."[21] In transitions of this nature, authoritarian leaders have not necessarily become democrats, but simply want to install a political system that can be accepted by the majority of the international community and so reduce external pressure.

Following the election, Thein Sein took office as the head of the first ostensibly civilian government in Burma for forty-nine years, and, despite the undemocratic election that had propelled him to power, announced that he was, in fact, preparing to lead the country toward democracy.

FREE AT LAST

On the afternoon of November 13, 2010, less than one week after the anticlimactic general election, reports had begun to circulate that the Burmese government was finally going to free Suu Kyi from the house arrest she had served for more than seven continuous years, and so both youth and senior leaders of the NLD began hastily preparing to welcome their beloved leader. Suddenly, the eyes and ears of Burma were focused on Suu Kyi's residence in Rangoon.

Several hundred meters up the road from Suu Kyi's lakeside home, thousands of her supporters gathered behind barbed-wire barricades to wait for the Nobel laureate's release, and thousands more streamed in that direction. Small groups intermittently approached the barricades and shouted, "Long live Daw Aung San Suu Kyi!"—*Daw* being a term of respect for a Burmese woman. Some supporters wore T-shirts reading, "We stand with Aung San Suu Kyi," "We love Suu," or "Freedom from Fear." While in

NLD headquarters, Rangoon. This photo was taken just before Suu Kyi's release in November 2010. The banner reads, "Only two days to go to free Daw Aung San Suu Kyi."

most countries this would be an innocuous show of support for a political leader, in Burma it constituted a brave act of political defiance, because wearing a T-shirt with a photo of Suu Kyi, or the words "democracy" or "freedom," printed on it would likely send the person wearing that T-shirt to prison. The gate to Suu Kyi's house—still closed and guarded by junta security officers—was surrounded by members of the local and international media, including those foreign journalists who were either working in Burma already or had been lucky enough to gain visas by pretending to be tourists.

The Irrawaddy's own undercover reporters in the crowd fed information on a minute-by-minute basis back to our newsroom in Chiang Mai, Thailand, where we rapidly placed the breaking news on both our Burmese- and English-language websites, and waited to capture the moment when Suu Kyi, who people were now referring to as "Amay Suu," or Mother Suu, emerged from years of forced seclusion.

Bearing in mind the regime's history of trumping up charges to keep Suu

Kyi imprisoned, and with still no definitive word by midafternoon that she would be released, the people outside her residence maintained a patient attitude up until the last minute. Even British Ambassador Andrew Heyn, who quietly showed up outside Suu Kyi's house hours before her release, remained cautious, saying, "We're just keeping our fingers crossed like everybody else."[22] Suu Kyi's supporters in the crowd were also hoping that the long-anticipated event would not turn into a tragic military crackdown. Truckloads of riot police cruised the streets and parked at major intersections—a familiar sight to Rangoon residents during times of political tension—and undercover intelligence officers took photographs of supporters and onlookers. But although the people were anxious, the atmosphere was calm and everyone waited peacefully.

There was no way for Suu Kyi to know exactly what was happening outside, however, and when she looked out the window and saw armed military and police troops holding automatic rifles, she thought they were ready to attack the crowd as they had done during the 1988 uprising and the 2007 Saffron Revolution. But neither the troops nor Suu Kyi's supporters initiated a confrontation and in the late afternoon, after military jeeps carrying Police Chief Brigadier General Khin Yee drove into the compound, riot police began removing the barricades and barbed wire, to the cheers of the crowd. Now believing Suu Kyi's release was imminent, her supporters flooded into the street and ran towards the gate.

Although details of the conversation that took place between Suu Kyi and Khin Yee are not known, it was reportedly a cordial meeting, with the police chief saying he was pleased to see that Suu Kyi was healthy. He also told the pro-democracy leader that he wanted to see a peaceful and stable Burma, and Suu Kyi said she hoped for the same.[23] After the formal pleasantries had been exchanged, Khin Yee read a statement from the Home Ministry stating that Suu Kyi was free and her prison sentence had been pardoned due to good behavior during detention. Suu Kyi's two female assistants Khin Khin Win and Win Ma Ma were also released and pardoned from identical eighteen-month sentences.

Finally, the moment both Suu Kyi and her supporters had waited years to enjoy arrived. Accompanied by her aides, "Mother Suu" left her house at approximately 5:45 p.m., and, wearing a lilac blouse, appeared at the perimeter fence before what was now estimated to be more than five thousand supporters. The crowd cheered wildly and chanted, "Long live Daw Aung San Suu Kyi!" and "We love Suu!" Many broke into tears of happiness, some waved to the soldiers as they left the compound, and those in front tried to reach out and shake their beloved leader's hand. "I'm very happy to see you all again," she finally said over the nonstop cheers and chants. "We haven't seen each other for so long, and I have so much to tell you."[24] One of Suu Kyi's supporters presented her with a flower, and when the crowd pleaded, "Put it in your hair," she smiled and complied. Everyone familiar with Suu Kyi recognized this as a signature moment; The Lady loves to wear flowers on any occasion. "Please have understanding with each other," Suu Kyi continued. "Let's work hand in hand. If we are united we can get what we want." The crowd then broke into an impromptu rendition of the Burmese national anthem, and at that moment it became clear to all that Suu Kyi had instantly reemerged as a national leader, despite being cut off from her people for more than seven years.

As is always the case in Burma, however, lurking behind the scenes were the junta generals: the same ruthless military clique who had nullified the NLD's overwhelming victory in the 1990 election, placed Suu Kyi under house arrest three times and, just the previous Sunday, orchestrated a sham election intended by almost all objective accounts to perpetuate military rule under the guise of a parliamentary system.

As Suu Kyi spoke, junta intelligence officers once again nervously took pictures of supporters, onlookers, and journalists. Win Tin later joked that the large crowd would make it difficult for intelligence officers to find photos of the gathering to present to regime leaders in Naypyidaw. "I think they are worried that the generals will have high blood pressure when they see pictures of Suu Kyi speaking to such a large crowd,"[25] he said.

Even though everyone was able to smile temporarily at the sight of Suu Kyi walking free, the question soon became how the generals would react to the overwhelming show of support she had received, which turned her release into an international event that overshadowed Burma's first general election in twenty years. Ironically, five days after the military-sponsored election, Suu Kyi was treated as if she were the landslide winner even though she had been excluded from participating in the polls.

While the crowds Suu Kyi drew may have given the generals indigestion, the attention her freedom received from the media may actually have been just what the junta intended. Her release clearly served to distract the press and the international community from the rigged polls held the week before. Some analysts concluded that it made perfect sense for the generals to free Suu Kyi at this time, since she was now no longer an electoral threat to them. In addition, having imprisoned her twice before, the generals probably felt they could detain Suu Kyi again at any time in the future, and, therefore, were in full control of the situation and ready to face down the devotion she still commanded both among the people of Burma and among Western supporters.

As the election demonstrated, however, Than Shwe would leave nothing to chance when it came to retaining his iron grip on the nation. The junta chief appeared to have carefully calculated that the political risk of freeing Suu Kyi was worth taking as long as he could silence her once again in the future if necessary. Well aware of this, minutes after Suu Kyi's release some of her supporters voiced concern for her personal safety and raised the possibility of a future assassination attempt. Their real fear was that she could become a martyr like her father, or, more recently, like Benazir Bhutto, Pakistan's slain opposition leader. When asked the next day whether she was concerned for her own safety, Suu Kyi replied, "I am a Burmese citizen and my security depends on the leaders of the nation."[26]

Despite the overwhelming show of support for Suu Kyi, the generals could take heart from the fact that her release did not prove to be the catalyst for an instant uprising. Nevertheless, for the overwhelming majority of Burmese people, November 13, 2010 is thought of as an exceptional day in Burmese history on which democracy began to take root once again. Suu Kyi's release provided them with the hope, expectation, and inspiration that they had lacked for many years. Given the inherent tension between the regime, which demands loyalty through ruthless oppression and swift punishment to those who openly oppose it, and

Suu Kyi, who commands loyalty by virtue of her personal qualities and universal ideals, nobody was sure how much political operating space the junta would allow her. But based on past history, she was certain at some point to test their limits.

Prior to her release, rumors circulated in Burma that Suu Kyi and regime officials had entered tense negotiations, with the regime insisting on a conditional release and Suu Kyi refusing any such conditions. So, without any clear rules established about what she could and could not do, the day after her release Suu Kyi went to NLD headquarters, where she first met with NLD leaders, addressed the thousands of supporters who had come to listen to her speak, and finally met with the press. According to Ohn Kyaing, now a senior member of the NLD, Suu Kyi's first words at the meeting of NLD leaders were, "I want to listen to the people of Burma's voices. I want to obey the people's wishes. So I want to engage in activities that put me in touch with the people." He said that Suu Kyi later discussed future activities, and the most significant topic she raised was her desire to make the NLD a "people's network," and develop a wide following as soon as possible.[27] Win Tin, who had recently been released from nineteen years in Insein Prison, said, "I met her for the first time in more than twenty years . . . she is exactly who I met in 1988: as energetic and enthusiastic as ever. She is well prepared to lead [the party] and I was impressed by her ideas, thoughts, and moral character. She will reclaim the hearts of the people."[28]

When the meeting with her NLD colleagues was over, Suu Kyi then proceeded to do just that, captivating the large crowd whose sheer number demonstrated the deep desire of the Burmese people to live freely in a democratic society, and giving a polite reminder to her former captors that, "Democracy is a system that allows the majority of people to guide a small group of people in power. . . . The rulers must be under the control of the people; I also wish to be controlled."[29] To thunderous applause, she then told her supporters that she would continue to work towards national reconciliation, particularly between the various pro-democracy opposition and ethnic groups. Suu Kyi also pointedly noted that the people themselves must actively participate in order to achieve their democratic goals, saying, "We cannot just 'work for people.' The people must also work. All must be brave enough to side with the truth. Every individual has an obligation."[30] She added that these goals would not be achieved easily, and that people must have courage and become willing to make sacrifices for the continuing struggle for democracy against the regime.

When she met the press, Suu Kyi pledged to continue to participate in a political movement, whether the NLD party existed or was disbanded. She said that the NLD was not a social welfare organization, and would remain a political organization. Controversially, she added that she intended to lead what she called a "nonviolent revolution," justifying her use of the term "revolution" by arguing, "I think of evolution as imperceptible change, very, very slowly, and I think of revolution as significant change. I say this because we are in need of significant change."[31]

A large crowd gathers around Aung San Suu Kyi at NLD headquarters for her first public speech after her release from house arrest (November 2010).

She noticeably did not call for regime change, as some of her supporters have done. "What we want is value change," she said. "Regime change can be temporary, but value change is a long-term business. We want the values in our country to be changed. We want a sound foundation for change. Even if there's regime change, if these basic values have not changed, then one regime change can lead to another regime change and so on and so on." Indicating that she would continue her call for dialogue with the military rulers, Suu Kyi said she did not harbor resentment towards the generals who had held her captive for fifteen of the past twenty-one years, and there was nobody, including Than Shwe, with whom she was not willing to talk. "I want to meet and talk with him [Than Shwe] directly. It would be very good if I could discuss with him whatever issues I care about," she said.[32]

APRIL 1 BY-ELECTIONS

After the rigged November 2010 elections that propelled new president Thein Sein into power, there were doubts that the president would be able to carry out a democratic governance of much legitimacy. But following meetings with American Secretary of State Hilary Clinton and the release of Aung San Suu Kyi and many other political prisoners, the government announced that by-elections for forty-five seats in Burma's 664-seat union parliament were to be held on April 1, 2012. Despite the less than auspicious date, euphoria swept the nation as anticipatation of an NLD landslide built. All eyes from the international community were on Burma, and famous correspondents from the BBC and CNN who had just arrived in Rangoon struggled to pronounce the names of the key protagonists. How the government would conduct the ballot was seen as a barometer of its commitment to political reform.

Prior to the vote, several international observers including the EU and the United States were allowed to monitor proceedings and subsequently praised the process as free and fair. However, there were notes of caution and an undercurrent of anxiety since everyone knew that even a complete victory would not bring meaningful change to the country.

In fact, the NLD secured less than 7 percent of the overall number of seats in the parliamentary union assembly's lower and upper houses, despite winning thirty-three of the thirty-four seats they contested. Nevertheless, Suu Kyi said she hoped the polls marked the start of a new era in Burma, and many countries, including the United States, voiced the opinion that the vote was an important step in Burma's transition to democracy. "The success we are having is the success of the people," Suu Kyi said in her victory speech. "It is not so much our triumph as a triumph of the people who have decided that they have to be involved in the political process in this country."[33]

The NLD claimed thirty-seven seats in the 440-member lower house, four in the upper house and two in regional chambers. Their sole loss was in eastern Shan State where the Shan Nationalities Democratic Party claimed victory, largely due to its huge support among the area's ethnic minorities. Although Suu Kyi herself received a large proportion of ethnic Karen votes in her own constituency. The USDP managed to claim a sole victory out of the forty-five constituencies contested, a seat in Burma's northwest Sagaing Division where the NLD candidate had been disqualified.

Once the results of the election were announced, the NLD was presented with a dilemma before it even entered parliament. Elected MPs for Burma's main opposition party were required to take a parliamentary oath to "uphold and abide" by the sham 2008 constitution. This stirred up debate both in and outside the country, and Suu Kyi wrote a letter to Thein Sein to request that the constitution be altered. The president, who was visiting Japan at the time, was quoted by *The Associated Press* upon receiving the letter as saying that Suu Kyi was welcome in parliament but "she is the one who should decide whether or not to join."[34]

This indecision and uncertainty on behalf of Suu Kyi did not sit well with critics. Min Zin, a Burmese scholar based in the United States, wrote,

> This is an unfortunate strategic blunder for the leader of the NLD. She has put herself in an unnecessary dilemma. First of all, the point at hand is largely symbolic. Semantic issues in politics are usually about saving face. Vowing to "uphold and abide" the constitution

does not mean that the opposition can't try to amend it later. A quick look at the texts of other countries' oaths of office shows that words like "uphold" and even "defend" are commonly used, but such language has never prevented anyone from proposing constitutional amendments.[35]

Critics accused the NLD of stalling over a minor issue, but many hardcore party members and supporters steadfastly continued to back this principled stance. Ordinary Burmese people who were expecting the NLD to enter parliament and highlight the substantial issues facing the country remained hugely disappointed, with many asking whether Suu Kyi had even studied the constitution. Finally, in May, Suu Kyi made the pragmatic decision to take the oath, along with forty-two other newly elected NLD members.

The free and fair April 1 by-elections seemed to mark a substantial leap towards democracy in Burma. Nevertheless, many skeptics commented that the election may simply have been a method with which to lure Suu Kyi and the other leaders of the NLD to take a step back from their influential dissident roles and to take up their parliamentary seats in Naypyidaw, where, with just a 7 percent hold on power, they would have little control in the governing of the country.

Regardless of the motives, however, and the consequences, it appeared that winning a landslide victory in the by-elections was a sign that, if left unfettered, the NLD could win a huge majority in the general election in 2015. The victory in 2012 was a wake-up call to the ruling USDP and military leaders that they could no longer cheat the people of Burma, and that the democracy movement inside Burma was not short of support.

2

THE COMRADES

I'm not going to be able to do it alone. One person alone can't do anything as important as bringing genuine democracy to a country.[1]

Upon her release from house arrest, Aung San Suu Kyi used these words to challenge each and every citizen of Burma to actively participate in the effort to bring democracy and a respect for human rights to the country. She urged the people to create a grass-roots political movement and placed a strong emphasis on forming a national people's network that could effectively pressure the junta leaders to change and—maybe just as importantly—convince lower-level military leaders to support their cause. In addition to entreating the support of ordinary Burmese people, however, to be able to bring about lasting change in Burma, Suu Kyi will also need to enlist the support of all of the colleagues she has worked with in the past and those who became active while she was placed under house arrest, as well as members of the many influential but disparate groups within the country. This may not be a simple task: each group has its own agenda, and while Suu Kyi was silenced during her years of house arrest the opposition movement became increasingly fractured and stagnant, with little communication and a great lack of trust between factions, and a host of ideologies on how to acheive democracy.

The main political group she must enlist, undoubtedly, are the elderly leaders of the NLD, whose members are known as the "uncles," and who worked closely with Suu Kyi whenever she was not under house arrest. They consist of former generals, politicians, and government officials who previously worked with Ne Win's socialist government. Despite their high status, they are particularly unpopular with the youth wing of the NLD and are also not highly regarded among the Burmese public.

Although not a political party, the 88 Generation Students group also holds political clout within Burma. Its members comprise former well-respected student leaders who were involved in the 1988 uprising, and many of whom served lengthy jail terms as a result, although many also remained active while Suu Kyi was under house arrest. The 88 Generation Students group was only formed by name after they were released from jail in 2004 and 2005. The group includes prominent members such as Min Ko Naing and Ko Ko Gyi.

Within Burma, Suu Kyi must also enlist the support of Burma's huge population of disenfranchised and persecuted ethnic minorities, the sangha, and other leading Burmese social activists. As well as the various groups inside Burma, the international community is keeping a close eye on developments in the country, and Suu Kyi must balance her own country's needs with the wishes of the UN and other outside parties.

Unifying all of these groups into one single mission is a huge challenge. Bringing these leaders and the diverse groups they represent together and forming a unified voice for change will be one of Suu Kyi's major leadership tasks as she tries to bring genuine democracy to Burma.

THE NATIONAL LEAGUE FOR DEMOCRACY

When Suu Kyi formed the NLD after the 1988 uprising, she initially organized the party as a league consisting of three factions: the Intellectuals, the Patriotic Old Comrades, and the Association of Nationalist Army Commanders, led by herself, prominent member Tin Oo, and former military general Aung Gyi, respectively. Soon after he was instated as a leader, however, Aung Gyi began accusing fellow party members of being communists, so the NLD's Central Executive Committee called an emergency meeting and voted to expel him and most of his followers, aside from a few, such as the influential Kyi Maung. This left Suu Kyi and Tin Oo heading the two remaining factions. Suu Kyi's faction, the intellectual wing of the party, had journalist and writer Win Tin as its leading member, whereas Tin Oo's faction consisted of former military officers such as himself and Aung Shwe. Both of these men were tasked with taking the reigns of the NLD while Suu Kyi and the other leaders were imprisoned, and despite Tin Oo's own imprisonment prior to the 1990 election. In their own way, all of these NLD leaders have left their mark on the party, and for better or worse, with the exception of Kyi Maung who died in 2004, they all continue to hold leadership positions.

One of the most important issues facing Suu Kyi now she has emerged from house arrest is how to balance her respect for the elders of her party, while at the same time move it forward by developing a new generation of leaders and incorporating modern resistance methods into the opposition's repertoire. In order to understand where she is leading the party, however, it is important to understand where it has been. This means becoming familiar with the three men who have been Suu Kyi's closest colleagues since the party was formed in 1988.

WIN TIN

Suu Kyi's right-hand man, Win Tin's journalistic background stretches all the way back to 1952, when he became chief editor of *The Oway*, a Burmese magazine, and also worked for *Agence France-Presse*. From 1954 to 1957, he worked at the Jumbarton newspaper company in the Netherlands as an advisory editor and also published a newsletter called *Doh Pyi Thadin* (Our Country's News) that was issued twice a week and distributed to Burmese living overseas.[2] Burma's intelligence service soon found out about the newsletter's existence, however, and, suspecting it contained

Win Tin stands with NLD supporters waiting for Suu Kyi to be released from house arrest (November 2010).

antigovernment material, sent an official to persuade him to stop the publication. When Win Tin refused he was called back to Burma.

Despite the government's attempt to clamp down on Win Tin's overseas newsletter, the country's 1947 constitution, in fact, guaranteed citizens the right to express their opinions and convictions, and Burma enjoyed perhaps the liveliest free press in Southeast Asia during the 1950s and early 1960s. This relative press freedom did not last long after Ne Win's coup in 1962, however, and the country's newspapers were soon nationalized, many foreign news agencies were asked to pack their bags, the Burma Journalist Association ceased to exist, and many journalists and editors found themselves in prison.

It was in this environment that Win Tin became chief editor of the Mandalay-based *Hanthawaddy* newspaper in 1968. Ne Win wanted full control over *Hanthawaddy*, and whenever the general traveled to Mandalay he would invite Win Tin to meet him at the old palace. Win Tin, however, refused once again to bow to the wishes of those in power, and in 1978, *Hanthawaddy* was shut down by the regime.

For the next ten years, Win Tin worked as a freelance writer and translator during a time when, despite the fact that Burma's new 1974 constitution also guaranteed freedom of expression, all publications and forms of public communication had to pass through Burma's notorious censorship board.

Later, during the period of the mass uprising in 1988, the people of Burma witnessed a brief revival of press freedom, and hundreds of pro-democracy bulletins, newspapers, and pamphlets began to be published without going through the censorship board. Newspapers and journals began to dig for inside stories of the socialist regime and aggressively competed to publish the latest news on Burma and its political upheaval. Even Burma's state-owned newspapers departed from the rose-tinted official line and began to deliver objective news reports and analysis.

Win Tin's spirit of independent journalism was reborn during this brief renaissance. He helped to edit several daily and weekly journals, and was behind the *Thamaga*, the student union newsletter that came out regularly during the crucial month of September 1988.

This new era of press freedom, however, was extremely short-lived, and in October 1989, SLORC officers raided Win Tin's house and used the "leftist literature" they seized to accuse him of being a communist, despite the fact that all of the books displayed at the press briefing on Win Tin's arrest could be bought at any second-hand book shop in Rangoon. He was sentenced to three years imprisonment and became the first NLD leader to spend time in Insein Prison. As the regime reportedly believed that Win Tin was the brains behind Suu Kyi's nonviolent struggle, it was not surprising that he was their first target.

A few days after being sentenced, two intelligence officers took Win Tin out of the prison without informing him where he was going. As it turned out, the army officers took him to see a propaganda exhibition called "The Real Story Under the Big Waves and Strong Winds," that the junta was holding in the Envoy Hall in Rangoon. The exhibition denounced the 1988 uprising, accusing those involved of attempting to create instability in the country, and claiming that the armed forces now had to shoulder the responsibility of saving the country. After he had seen the exhibition, the intelligence officers asked him whether he was interested in joining the junta. Win Tin shook his head. They then gave him a pen and paper and asked him to write his opinion of the exhibition. Win Tin wrote a twenty-five-page critique of the display, with the punchline being that "the duty of the armed forces is to go back to the barracks." The intelligence officers were furious. Afterwards, they regularly took him for interrogation—always wearing a hood—and often subjected him to physical torture and humiliation. On some occasions, Win Tin would be placed on a chair near other hooded political prisoners, some his colleagues, who were making confessions about the NLD and Suu Kyi, and even about him. The intelligence officers wanted Win Tin to be aware that other NLD members were collaborating with the junta.

Win Tin and his fellow prisoners were hungry for news from the outside, but they were prohibited from listening to radios and reading books inside prison. Even so, some of his fellow prisoners smuggled shortwave radios, codenamed "parrots," into the prison and hid them in the prison walls. Whenever he had the chance, Win Tin would speak to those prisoners with access to parrots to get an update on what they had heard from the BBC and VOA.

In 1992, when the SLORC chairman, Senior General Saw Maung, was "permitted to resign" due to health reasons, Than Shwe offered conditional amnesty to political prisoners. In exchange for their freedom, several prisoners signed an agreement not to take part in politics again. But Win Tin did not. He believed that staying in prison was his duty as a political activist, did not plea for his release, and also sent a secret message to his colleagues persuading them not sign the agreement either. In response, the regime extended Win Tin's sentence by ten years.

It was then that Win Tin began publishing an underground newspaper from his prison cell, entitled *The Tidal Wave*—an activity that risked yet another seven years imprisonment on top of his lengthy sentence. Sympathetic guards smuggled in radios, books, pens, paper, and colored pencils, and Win Tin wrote articles on current political questions as well as the contemporary history of Burmese political science.

While some angry and frustrated political prisoners lashed out at figureheads such as Suu Kyi during this period, Win Tin remained a faithful and loyal supporter. Rather than attacking Suu Kyi, he led the way and demonstrated to the other prisoners how to confront the regime. As a result, Win Tin gained huge respect in prison and became as admired as Suu Kyi by many young activists and students.

Despite his loyalty to Suu Kyi, Win Tin did not follow her blindly. When she was facing the bogus charge of harboring an American swimmer at her lakeside house in 2009, a frustrated Win Tin said,

Suu Kyi is a VIP prisoner—we spent our times in dog cells[*] and we were treated inhumanely. Our feeling and sentiment toward the generals is not the same as Aung San Suu Kyi. She always looked at them with some understanding and she sees the military as her father's army. But we don't.[3]

While he was imprisoned, he was often visited by diplomats, US congressmen, International Committee of the Red Cross (ICRC) officials, and UN human rights investigators. In his book, *What's That? A Human Hell?*, published in Burmese, Win Tin recalled a 1994 meeting with US Congressman Bill Richardson, who also met Suu Kyi. In front of intelligence officers holding tape recorders, Win Tin did not hesitate to tell the congressman that the military-sponsored national constitutional convention was a sham process and that a boycott was the only solution. When Richardson asked what message Win Tin had for Suu Kyi, he replied just, "Stay the course."[4]

In 1995, Brigadier General Than Tun, the then head of the government counterintelligence unit, came to the prison just before the fiftieth anniversary of the Burmese Armed Forces Day and asked Win Tin to sign a

---

[*]The dog cells at Insein Prison are approximately ten feet long and seven feet wide, with a small window, and soundproof. There is generally no proper sanitation, no bed, and no mats on the floor. Prison officials sometimes keep political prisoners in dog cells to punish them if they break prison rules, or are involved in political activities or hunger strikes.

Criminal Procedure Code Section 401 (CPC 401), a law used by the regime to reduce the sentence of political prisoners in exchange for their agreement to abide by terms set by the regime. Knowing that the regime wanted to free him as a propaganda ploy, Win Tin refused to sign. Than Tun was livid and had Win Tin thrown out of the room.[5]

After five years in prison, Win Tin celebrated his sixty-fifth birthday by giving a speech that he shouted out loudly from his cell so that other prisoners could hear in their own 10-by-8-by-12-foot cells. Zin Linn, a Burmese writer who was also in Insein Prison at the time, recalled Win Tin's words:

> The junta put us in dog cells to crush our morale, but by doing so our spirits have been hardened and tempered. It is a pity that they don't even know the law of nature. A true politician will do his best, wherever he is, whether in parliament or in prison. His duty is to implement the will of his nation. To consider the nation's future is the most important duty of all of us, even while we are in prison. The dictators can detain only our bodies, but not our souls.[6]

The same year, Win Tin and his colleagues conducted a clandestine mission to collect information on human rights violations inside Insein Prison. Win Tin edited the eighty-three-page report, entitled "Human Rights Abuses in the Junta's Prisons," and smuggled it out to Yozo Yokota, the UN special rapporteur for Burma.

It was shortly after this, at midnight on September 11, 1995, that prison authorities raided prisoners' cells in a surprise search. They dug up the concrete floors and found underground casings containing books, papers, pens, colored pencils, two radios, news bulletins, and some small tools. Sixty-three inmates were taken, handcuffed, and put into solitary confinement, while eight, including Win Tin, were sent to the hellish dog cells. Despite having just been discharged from hospital, he was forced to sleep on a concrete floor and denied drinking water for two full days. In March 1996, twenty-four political prisoners, including Win Tin, received an additional seven plus years in prison in a closed trial.

Six years later, in 2001, and while still behind bars, Win Tin was awarded the UNESCO/Guillermo Cano World Press Freedom Prize for his efforts to defend and promote the right to freedom of expression. The same year, he was also awarded the World Association of Newspapers' Golden Pen of Freedom Award.

In 2002, ICRC officials informed Win Tin that they were entering into negotiations with the regime to free some elderly and sick political prisoners, but Win Tin refused the assistance, telling them he wanted to be released as a political prisoner, not as a sick or elderly prisoner.[7]

In October 2004, Khin Nyunt and his entire Military Intelligence Service were purged. Khin Nyunt received a forty-four-year suspended sentence for insubordination and corruption, and around forty of his former associates and members of his dismantled intelligence agency were sentenced to prison terms ranging from twenty to one hundred years. Among those facing the heaviest sentences was none other than Than Tun, the man who had berated Win Tin for refusing to sign the CPC 401 nine years previously. As a result, Win Tin and Than Tun met in Insein Prison for the second time, but on this occasion both were behind bars. Win Tin could walk out of his own cell in the daytime—a small freedom considered a reward in the prison—so he once walked past Than Tun's cell and saw the ex-junta official sitting quietly, looking withdrawn, perhaps pondering how he was going to survive his lengthy prison sentence in the presence of so many enemies. In any case, the formerly powerful intelligence officer would not look the NLD leader in the eye.

Than Tun was not the only formerly powerful player that Win Tin met behind prison walls. In 2008, he also met Ne Win's grandson Aye Ne Win, who, along with his father and brother had been arrested on charges of planning a coup and sentenced to death. He found the young man, then in his early thirties, to be polite, calm, and educated. Aye Ne Win's mother would send him books and Win Tin often borrowed them, even having the chance to finish *Harry Potter*. And when they discussed issues about Burma, Win Tin was surprised to learn they saw many things eye to eye. Aye Ne Win often expressed his deep respect for Suu Kyi, whom he called "Aunty

Suu," and also said he hoped that student leader Min Ko Naing would be freed, although he also insisted he was not interested in party politics.

In February 2008, a senior police officer came to the prison at a time when Win Tin was receiving medication and asked him once again to sign the CPC 401, fourteen years after it was last presented to him. Win Tin remained unbowed and shouted at the officer to leave the room immediately.[8] The international community, however, kept pressing the regime to free the iron-willed Win Tin, who was often reported to have died due to ill health and mistreatment.

Finally, on September 23, 2008, prison officials, seemingly having run out of options for an official release on their terms, took Win Tin out of his room, put him in a car, and dropped him off at his friend's house not far from Insein. The officials then quickly left the scene to avoid the large crowd that would soon arrive to welcome their idol, who, still wearing a blue-colored prison uniform, was now a free man after spending nineteen years in prison.

Win Tin is a real activist, but he is not a traditional politician. He spent over seven thousand nights in Insein Prison with no regrets, carrying the pro-democracy flag and helping keep the opposition movement alive. Political pundits speculated about the timing of Win Tin's release, wondering whether it had come about because the regime had finally given in to the fiery intellectual's steadfastness, because of international pressure, or possibly for more strategic reasons. The regime had already announced plans to hold a general election at some point in the future, and the junta leaders may have calculated that Win Tin would take a hard-line stance against the election and further the regime's agenda of splintering the NLD.

If that was what they intended, the generals were presciently correct, because that is exactly what happened. Win Tin declined the offer to be reinstated into his old position as secretary of the NLD, but at the age of seventy-nine he rejoined the Central Executive Committee, reassuming his status as one of the party's leading members. In the process, he reinvigorated the NLD and inspired many people inside and outside Burma by taking a clear stand against the regime and its sham election.

TIN OO

A former prominent member of Burma's armed forces with a military background that stretches all the way back to the fight for independence, Tin Oo also spent many years as a political prisoner.

Tin Oo (February 2011)

The head of the Patriotic Old Comrades faction and former vice-chairman of the NLD was once a faithful soldier who rapidly rose to the top ranks of the military. He joined the armed forces in 1943 when he was only sixteen years old and was a lieutenant by 1947, the year that saw the assassination of his hero, Aung San. Following independence, Tin Oo won the Thura* award twice during the fight against Kuomintang troops in northern Burma, and in 1964 he became commander of the Central Command. The year 1974 marked the pinnacle of his military career when he became both Ne Win's defense minister and commander-in-chief of the armed forces.

---

*The third-highest award in Burma's armed forces

At the time, Tin Oo had absolute faith in Ne Win and the "Burmese Way to Socialism." He once told his aides that it was important to protect Ne Win because the longer the dictator lived, the better it would be for Burma.[9] So, when protests broke out in 1974 following a crackdown on students who had hijacked the coffin of U Thant, the recently deceased UN secretary-general, Tin Oo ordered his forces to violently suppress the demonstrations. Tin Oo later spoke about that day: "As the defense chief I was forced to fire on people, gun people down," he said. "This was the policy. I followed it blindly."[10]

In 1976, there was another outbreak of student protests and the government closed down the colleges and universities. They were reopened shortly afterwards and Tin Oo was this time hailed as a champion of the people, with students shouting, "Long Live Tin Oo!" These chants undoubtedly reached Ne Win's ears through the powerful intelligence service that reported directly to him, and shortly afterwards the dictator betrayed his loyal armed forces chief, forcing him to resign on March 6, 1976. The official reason for Tin Oo's involuntary retirement was that his wife, Dr. Tin Moe Wei, had broken the rules laid down for the spouses of commanding officers by accepting numerous bribes. Tin Oo was, in fact, building a house at that time and army sources said his family did ask a Burmese military attaché serving overseas to send housing materials. But this was common practice among top leaders and many observers speculated that the real reason behind Tin Oo's sacking was his growing popularity among the rank and file of the armed forces and the general public.

In typically callous style, Ne Win's officers informed the outgoing commander-in-chief that he was being removed from his post during a religious ceremony for his recently deceased youngest son. None of this sat well with Tin Oo's closest supporters, and as a result, a group led by Captain Ohn Kyaw Myint plotted to assassinate Ne Win and other state leaders on Armed Forces Day. After persuading several regional officers and ministers to be part of the plan, the captain went to see Tin Oo and told him about the plot. While Tin Oo asked him to abort the mission, the other mutineers went forward with what turned out to be an ill-conceived and ill-planned assassination attempt.[11] News of the plot leaked to Ne Win's intelligence unit and Captain Ohn Kyaw Myint was arrested, along with a dozen other army officers. In July 1977, he was sentenced to death by a tribunal and hanged.

Tin Oo was also arrested in connection with the plot and held for withholding information about the abortive coup plan. His pensions and benefits were cut off and he was sent to Insein Prison, where he served seven years in harsh conditions. He once said that in solitary confinement he felt like a caged, enraged animal, and he began to practice meditation and mindfulness while behind bars.[12]

After being given amnesty in 1981, he went straight to the famous Mahasi Monastery to continue his studies. After two years he returned to a layman's life, studied law, received his degree, and stayed away from politics and Ne Win until 1988, when he resurfaced and joined the NLD, forming the Patriotic Old Comrades faction alongside other former military commanders and officers.

Along with Suu Kyi and most of the other NLD leaders, Tin Oo was imprisoned after the 8888 uprising from 1989 to 1995. He was again arrested along with Suu Kyi in 2003, after the government-backed mob attacked their motorcade in Depayin. He was initially held at a prison in Kalay, northwest Burma, but was brought back to Rangoon in February 2004 and placed under house arrest. Tin Oo's detention was extended every year thereafter, and he was denied access to visitors, including fellow party leaders, during his entire period of incarceration and house arrest. In early 2010, he was finally released and reassumed his position as vice-chairman of the NLD.

In contrast to the speculation about Win Tin's release, activists and politicians in Burma believe that Tin Oo was probably released because the regime believed his age and relative lack of popularity made him less of a threat during the upcoming polls than Suu Kyi. An ethnic Arakanese (Rakhine) leader confirmed this, saying in an interview about Win Tin's release, "He is a good leader for the NLD, but he's not as influential as Aung San Suu Kyi, so the military generals thought that he wouldn't be able to obstruct the upcoming elections."[13]

KYI MAUNG

Like Tin Oo, Kyi Maung was once in the upper echelons of Ne Win's regime. He was a commander in the army and a member of the dictator's revolutionary council, but was forced to retire because he opposed the 1962 coup and believed the military should not be involved in politics. He later spent seven years in prison while Ne Win was in power.

Kyi Maung was one of the few Aung Gyi followers who remained in the NLD after his faction was expelled. Despite the initial doubts that some party members had about his political integrity and his association with Aung Gyi, he went on to become a fine leader. Suu Kyi even gave him credit for guiding the NLD to its landslide victory in the May 1990 election following her arrest and that of Tin Oo and Win Tin.

Kyi Maung. Courtesy Nic Dunlop

In July 1990, the NLD leaders and elected MPs announced that they would hold a meeting in Rangoon's Gandhi Hall. Then, on July 27, just before the meeting took place, the SLORC issued its infamous Notification No. 1/90, a preemptive strike stating that only the SLORC had the right to exercise legislative, executive, and judicial powers, and that it would not accept a government formed under an interim constitution. It also stated that parties who had contested the election were to draw up guidelines for a new constitution, to convene a national convention, and to call for a referendum.

Despite the order, the NLD Central Executive Committee and all elected members of parliament from the NLD and its sister parties attended what came to be known as the Gandhi Conference, where they unanimously passed two key resolutions calling for the transfer of power to the NLD and the convening of parliament. Afterwards, Kyi Maung and the other NLD leaders expected an unavoidable political showdown, but instead what arrived was a military crackdown. On September 7, 1990, the junta arrested Kyi Maung and other top NLD leaders. He was tried by a military tribunal and sentenced to twenty years in prison.

Kyi Maung was released in 1994, but three years later he had a disagreement with Suu Kyi—the origins of which remain obscure to this day—and quit politics. This proved to be a major blow to the embattled NLD for several reasons. During his time with the party, Kyi Maung had proved to be a leader who could easily mingle with the party's younger generation, a group with which many other senior leaders did not spend time and to which they did not relate. In addition, with Suu Kyi and Tin Oo soon imprisoned once again, along with Win Tin, the NLD had no one as bold and charismatic as Kyi Maung to lead the party outside prison walls. The regime also took advantage of the split by accusing Suu Kyi of being an inflexible leader who had forced Kyi Maung to leave the party.

Neither Kyi Maung nor Suu Kyi ever revealed what disagreement happened between them, and in August 2004, Kyi Maung suffered a heart attack and died at his home in Rangoon at the age of eighty-five. Even after his death, however, Kyi Maung continued to inspire young dissidents. In August 2007, the 88 Generation Students leaders attended a religious ceremony at Kyi Maung's house on the anniversary of his death. When they left the gathering to protest the unannounced increase in fuel prices, they bypassed the bus station and marched along the road in what was the beginning, in effect, of the Saffron Revolution. Two days later, the 88

Generation Students' leaders were arrested and each given sixty-five-year-six-month prison sentences.

AUNG SHWE AND THE UNCLES

One long-time NLD leader who has been able to avoid prison is the party's former chairman, Aung Shwe, who is now in his nineties. His military and political credentials are impeccable. Before 1962, he was a brigadier general and commander of the Northern Command under Prime Minister U Nu, Burma's first democratically elected prime minister. He was also ambassador to Australia, France, and Egypt. Then, under Ne Win, he served as minister of finance and deputy prime minister, and was a member of the State Council until 1980.

After Ne Win resigned in 1988 and his government was deposed in the military coup, Aung Shwe joined the NLD. Then, in 1989, when Suu Kyi

Aung Shwe delivers his speech during the NLD's 18th anniversary celebration in Rangoon.

was placed under house arrest and other senior NLD leaders were also imprisoned, she appointed Aung Shwe treasurer and secretary of the party. He was known as a compromiser and was not media friendly; after Suu Kyi was released in 1995 she was forced to defend him from criticism for failing to push for political reform or to engage in any real activism while she was under house arrest. Accusations came not just from young party leaders and members, but from outside followers of the NLD and detached political observers, that Aung Shwe and the uncles had actually been detrimental to the movement while the other leaders were behind bars. To counter this, Suu Kyi argued, "Uncle U Aung Shwe tried very hard to keep the NLD together as well as trying to establish a harmonious relationship with the SLORC." She also addressed accusations that he lacked the will to take action while the other leaders were imprisoned, stating that these accusations were down to Aung Shwe's "gentlemanly"[14] manner.

Despite Suu Kyi's defense, Aung Shwe and the NLD leadership once again came under criticism during the 2007 Saffron Revolution, when

Senior members of the NLD at the party's 18th anniversary celebration at NLD headquarters (2006)

they were accused of failing to take an active role and work with the 88 Generation Students group. A report by the US embassy in Rangoon noted, "Already frustrated with the sclerotic leadership of the elderly NLD uncles, the party lost even more credibility within the pro-democracy movement when its leaders refused to support the demonstrators last September, and even publicly criticized them."[15] The report went on to say that repeated overtures from and meetings with the leaders of the 88 Generation Students group had not lead to any meaningful cooperation.[16]

Despite Suu Kyi's immense popularity while she was under house arrest, as a result of the uncles' cautious approach the NLD became estranged from both the younger generation of political activists and the ethnic minority groups. Suu Kyi perhaps relied on the uncles while she was absent because they all had connections to the armed forces. However, it has been proven over time that the retired generals have little influence on the army. Perhaps because, like Aung Shwe, many prominent NLD uncles are in their eighties and nineties.

In December 2009, while she was still under house arrest, Suu Kyi was allowed to meet three of these aging leaders, Aung Shwe, U Lwin, and Lun Tin, to pay her respects to them. When Suu Kyi asked them to allow her to reform and restructure the NLD, all agreed, and Suu Kyi sent a message to Win Tin telling him to reform the party.

It seems that Suu Kyi has little choice now she has been released but to keep the elderly uncles in positions of power for as long as they want to remain there. However, she will have to balance her respect for these figures with building much-needed bridges to the younger generation and nurturing those that are capable of stepping up to take on leadership roles from the aging uncles in the near future.

88 GENERATION STUDENTS

While the release of Suu Kyi was indeed cause for celebration, the people of Burma were acutely aware that she was but one of approximately twenty-two hundred political prisoners in Burma at the time. The country has forty-four prisons and more than one hundred labor camps where political prisoners are kept in poor conditions, with many having died since 1988 due to mistreatment. Despite the damning evidence, in October 2010, just prior to the election, the Burmese ambassador to the United Nations audaciously stated, "There are no political prisoners in Myanmar [Burma], and no individual has been incarcerated simply for his or her political beliefs."[17] This public denial was reiterated a year later in August 2011 by Burma's Chief Justice Tun Tun Oo.[18]

Some of the most prominent political prisoners, released only in January 2012, were the leaders of the 88 Generation Students group, including Min Ko Naing and Ko Ko Gyi. As students, these two men played a major role in the 1988 uprising and braved the bloodshed on the streets

Members of the 88 Generation Students group hold a press conference after the amnesty that resulted in their release from prison (January 2012).

at the time. Afterwards, they spent fifteen and fourteen years behind bars, respectively, in their initial stint as political prisoners. Upon their release in 2005, they formed the 88 Generation Students group and began conducting nonviolent activities that included visiting political prisoners' homes and holding commemoration ceremonies at Shwedagon Pagoda in Rangoon. But just two years later they were once again arrested, this time for organizing a protest against the steep rise in fuel prices before the Saffron Revolution. For this "crime" they were given identical sixty-five-year sentences and sent to separate remote prisons, where they then had little contact with the outside world.

While virtually unknown outside Burma, the 88 Generation Students group leaders may be just as significant as Suu Kyi to the future of the country. They represent a lost generation of pro-democracy political leaders in Burma, and the junta is well aware that their imprisonment left a void in opposition leadership that severely hindered its forces. The junta was also aware that while the release of Suu Kyi, who had become a well-known international figure, brought them cover for the stolen election and for criticism of the regimes repressive tactics, the release of Min Ko Naing and Ko Ko Gyi would have brought them a small fraction of the positive international attention that Suu Kyi's release received, while constituting a greater risk to the regime's grip on power.

Knowing that some of Burma's most promising young leaders were languishing in prison, Suu Kyi and the pro-democracy opposition would have been wise to have made their names and faces as recognizable to the international community as hers had become, and the "new" government's decision to release them was rightly considered a watershed moment that real change was occurring in the country. Their stories, both tragic and inspirational, should be known by all who care about Burma.

MIN KO NAING

Min Ko Naing (Conqueror of Kings) is the nom de guerre of Paw Oo Htun, who was born in Rangoon in 1962, the year the country's fledgling democracy fell to General Ne Win.

As a popular, artistically gifted student, he was an active member of the Rangoon Arts and Science University (RASU) arts club, where he enjoyed reading, writing poems, and drawing cartoons, especially satirical ones. Min Ko Naing was also a member of a performance troupe that performed plays and sketches satirizing Ne Win's regime, highlighting the lack of freedom and democracy in Burma, as well as corruption among its officials.

Min Ko Naing's troupe proved to be very popular with its audience of ordinary Burmese, but, predictably, it also attracted the attention of the dreaded Military Intelligence Service. Convinced that the time would soon be ripe for political change when the first signs of serious public unrest

Min Ko Naing (2006)

began to appear after Ne Win demonetized the one hundred kyat note, Min Ko Naing and his friends continued their satirical characterization of the country's deteriorating political, social, and economic conditions and secretly established an underground student union in anticipation of a political uprising.

On March 16, 1988, about three thousand students came to listen to the thin, dark-skinned young man with curly hair, a slight moustache, and beard give his first antigovernment speech at Taungoo dormitory on the RASU campus. He called on students to speak out against government mistreatment and informed them about the history of student movements in Burma and the role they have played in national politics: something the military government had ignored in their history textbooks. He also told his audience about the fate of earlier student movements that had challenged the present regime, saying, "Our brothers in the past sacrificed to topple this military dictatorship, but their demands were only met with violence, bullets, and killing."[19]

After continuing the speech at the Convocation Hall on the RASU campus, many of the students then left to join a small demonstration at the other major university, the RIT, only to come face to face with a barbed-wire barricade manned by dozens of soldiers on Prome Road. Confronted with this show of force, Min Ko Naing asked the students to sing the national anthem and salute Burma's independence heroes, including General Aung San. They shouted, "The peoples' soldiers are our soldiers!" and Min Ko Naing and two other students negotiated with the soldiers, stressing the importance of good relations between the army and the people. After a tense few minutes the soldiers lowered their guns. Suddenly, however, hundreds of riot police rushed in from behind and started beating the students. Some tried to escape their attackers by fleeing to nearby Inya Lake, where many drowned. Those who could not escape were severely beaten and taken to Insein Prison.

After this, the government closed down the universities and colleges, and Min Ko Naing and his fellow student activists went into hiding to continue their opposition activities. When the universities and colleges reopened in June, activists immediately began distributing antigovernment leaflets urging students to join their movement. Despite the fact that news of young students being tortured in Insein Prison spread all over the country, on the campuses the protests continued and the student movement gained momentum.

On June 12, 1988, a crowd of students formed on the university campus to look at copies of a poster drawn by Min Ko Naing that depicted a girl being beaten by soldiers near Inya Lake. The caption below the drawing said, "Don't forget March 16. If we are cowed into submission and fail to rise up this time, then the country will be ruled by even more repressive rulers in the future." Several students spoke out demanding the release of student activists and the reinstatement of students who had been expelled from universities for political reasons. Within a week, the government closed all universities and colleges again, but Min Ko Naing and his colleagues were able to evade the intelligence officers once more and stayed safe.

In July and August, hundreds of leaflets and poems signed by Min Ko Naing were secretly distributed in Rangoon, so many that it was hard to know which had been written by the real Min Ko Naing, or how many Min Ko Naings there actually were. In addition, millions in Burma were becoming familiar with his name through the BBC's Burmese Service. To the Burmese people, the name Min Ko Naing implied courage, commitment, and hope.

On August 8, 1988, the activist born under the name Paw Oo Tun officially became known as Min Ko Naing. Earlier that month he had issued a statement under the name of the All Burma Federation of Students' Unions (ABFSU), an organization that had played an important role in the struggle against colonial rule, calling for a general strike. So on that day, which later became known as the 8888 uprising, a sea of monks, workers, and students marched to Rangoon's City Hall. Then, in the afternoon, a large crowd gathered to listen to Min Ko Naing give a speech in front of the US embassy. "We, the people of Burma, have had to live without human dignity for twenty-six years under an oppressive rule. We must end dictatorial rule in our country. Only people power can bring down our repressive rulers," he told the crowd. Min Ko Naing concluded his speech by saying, "If we want to enjoy the same rights as people in other countries, we have to be disciplined, united, and brave enough to stand up to the dictators. Let's express our suffering and demands. Nothing is going to stop us from achieving peace and justice in our country."[20]

That night, the soldiers opened fire on demonstrators gathered in front of the City Hall and hundreds of people were gunned down. Troops were given the same orders in the provinces where even more died. The violence continued the next day, as crowds from around Rangoon converged to form huge masses demanding change. Once again, the soldiers opened fire killing hundreds of peaceful demonstrators.

Min Ko Naing spoke to a large audience in front of Rangoon General Hospital, the site of many recent killings, on August 23. Once again, the student leader called on people to be strong: "World history has shown that people with strong spirit, unity, courage and discipline can bring down authoritarian governments. We believe in people power. Without your participation, we can achieve nothing."[21]

On August 28, Burma's first student congress in twenty-six years was held on the RASU campus, and thousands of students, veteran politicians, and former student activists from the 1960s came to celebrate the official reestablishment of the ABFSU, with Min Ko Naing as its leader. He read one of his poems, entitled "Faith," in which he promised to be faithful and committed to the people's struggle, which he regarded as a fight for the truth. He took an oath that out of respect for those who had died before him, he would continue to fight until democracy and human rights were restored.

Rumor spread through the new student congress that on August 23, one day before martial law was lifted, a secret meeting had taken place at Ne Win's residence. Ne Win chaired the meeting that was reportedly attended by Sein Lwin, then commander-in-chief Dr. Maung Maung, Aye Ko, Prime Minister Thura Tun Tin, Kyaw Htin, Chief of Staff General Saw Maung, Intelligence Chief Khin Nyunt, and other senior cabinet ministers. The participants in this secret meeting decided to create chaos—if necessary using arson and assassination as weapons—and the army would use the worsening state of the country as a pretext for staging a coup.

The plan was carefully implemented. The day after a riot at Insein Prison thousands of convicts were freed, and, in hindsight, it became clear that the riot was state-sponsored and it was intended to spread to other jails. Criminal gangs poisoned a water supply tank in Rangoon, and looting and arson became a daily occurrence. The government's powerful intelligence units were behind all of this, and the furious public caught and beheaded criminal gang members in revenge.

Student leaders were aware that transportation and communication had come to a complete halt, and the Military Intelligence Service was trying to create anarchy by releasing criminals from the prisons. With criminals without food or money roaming the city and the brutal regime gunning down protesters, panic ensued in Rangoon with troops unwilling to intervene and assist the people. Min Ko Naing and his fellow students, along with the monks, shared the burden of attempting to control the situation, calming the public, and persuading them not to confront or physically harm the army or rioters.

After the coup, Min Ko Naing disappeared from public view for a few days. He was a prime target but he could not run away and was not interested in going to the border to take up arms. In a rare interview with *Asiaweek* magazine in late 1988, Min Ko Naing, who appeared on the cover wearing a mask, said, "I'll never die. Physically I might be dead, but many more Min Ko Naing will appear to take my place. As you know, Min Ko Naing can only conquer a bad king. If the ruler is good, we will carry him on our shoulders."[22]

While evading arrest, Min Ko Naing and his colleagues appeared at University Avenue to meet Suu Kyi, who had recently formed the NLD. While Suu Kyi usually asked people to make appointments to see her, Min Ko Naing and the other student leaders could meet her anytime. Suu Kyi knew that she and the student leaders were the only figures that both dared to defy the brutal regime and commanded public trust and faith, so she always welcomed them. Suu Kyi and Min Ko Naing were natural allies, but Min Ko Naing wanted to work under the student flag and felt that students, not politicians, were the ones who had sacrificed in the political struggle. Min Ko Naing and the other student leaders also continuously questioned Suu Kyi's political strategy. "What is your next step and your initiative?"[23] was the question Min Ko Naing would ask Suu Kyi whenever they debated the situation in Burma. Both knew there was no time to waste as both anticipated being put in prison.

On March 13, 1989, the then twenty-six-year-old Min Ko Naing gave his last public speech for many years at a gathering of thousands of students on the RIT campus, on the occasion of the first anniversary of the death of a student named Phone Maw. Min Ko Naing's speech criticized Ne Win and the military for that killing and the massacres that followed. His colleagues admired him for many reasons: one was his honesty, and another his public-speaking skills—he would usually employ simple, common language that people could absorb and understand. Ten days later, Min Ko Naing was arrested by the regime in anticipation of the protests that were going to be held to mark Armed Forces Day on March 27. Min Ko Naing was charged under section 5(j) of the 1950 Emergency Provisions Act for having delivered antigovernment speeches and agitating unrest. For this, he was sentenced to twenty years imprisonment in solitary confinement.

While other political prisoners were held in group cells and received regular family visits, and some even had their sentences reduced, Min Ko Naing was kept isolated and without any reduction of his sentence. There were great fears about his health, and his friends were concerned that his incredibly long period of solitary confinement must have been affecting his state of mind.[24] There were reports that he had suffered a serious nervous breakdown, and even that he had died. This was all speculation. However, there were also confirmed reports of torture. According to Amnesty International, Min Ko Naing was severely tortured and ill-treated during the early stages of his detention, and his health suffered as a consequence. During his interrogation, he was reportedly forced to stand in water until he collapsed, and as a result his left foot became totally numb.

In February 1994, US Congressman Bill Richardson visited Min Ko Naing in Insein Prison. While Richardson reportedly sought permission from the regime to take him to the United States, Min Ko Naing declined the offer, and instead conveyed a simple message to his friends: "Don't give up."

After spending twelve years in Insein Prison, Min Ko Naing was transferred to a prison in Sittwe, Arakan State, where he was allowed to read books. Then, on November 19, 2004, he was unexpectedly released after being imprisoned for fifteen years. He was then forty-two. A month later, after purging intelligence chief Khin Nyunt and his staff, the regime announced that it was freeing 3,937 prisoners, including Min Ko Naing, because they had been improperly sentenced by the Military Intelligence Service. Upon his release, Min Ko Naing just said, "I come back home like someone who has done his work."[25]

When the former student leaders, who by then were in their forties, were released from prison, they had matured and, to the surprise of many, were no longer divided and were willing to work together. They soon formed the 88 Generation Students group, and the network began a nationwide peaceful campaign to free political prisoners, collecting hundreds of thousands of signatures that were submitted to the regime and UN. As well as this, they launched several other campaigns including a mass multireligious prayer campaign, during which they urged people to wear white clothing and hold candlelit vigils in Buddhist, Christian, Hindu, and Muslim places of worship. The moral authority of the informal network of former students surprised the junta, as tens of thousands heeded the call and offered prayers for a peaceful resolution to Burma's political impasse and freedom for all political prisoners.

In early 2007, they commenced the successful Open Heart Movement, a campaign encouraging Burmese across the country to write letters about their everyday complaints and grievances with military rule. At the time, the 88 Generation Students were more effective than the NLD, and although the activities of their leaders were peaceful, as the group gained political momentum and the opposition movement became reinvigorated, the regime could no longer tolerate them.

The final straw came in 2007 when Min Ko Naing joined many others to protest the rise in fuel prices. Two days later, Min Ko Naing and his colleagues were snatched from their homes and locked up once again by the paranoid regime. They were later given long sentences and sent to various prisons, forceably ending their role in the democracy movement.

Five years later, in January 2012, Min Ko Naing and the other 88 Generation Students were released under the presidential pardon. The world applauded the government's gesture and welcomed them home. As expected, Min Ko Naing kept his head high when he walked out of prison. Crowds gathered to greet him and shouted, "Long Live Min Ko Naing!" and "good health!" His spirit seemed toughened, and he told supporters that his release was due to the will of the people. His popularity and determination have shown, once again, that he and his comrades can be the face of Burma's future. Their spirit of resistance is unbreakable.

KO KO GYI

"We have a long tradition of expecting the arrival of a king [to lead us in times of difficulty]," Ko Ko Gyi told a crowd of pro-democracy activists packed into a Rangoon house in 2007. "But democracy does not come from someone else. We ourselves must strive to achieve the thing which in English we call our 'birthright'."[26] Shortly after speaking these words, the man who is viewed as one of the main strategists behind Burma's student-led opposition groups found himself at Rangoon Airport, hands cuffed and legs in shackles, with a police officer using an iron chain to drag him to an airplane like a dog.

The Burmese military regime was shipping Ko Ko Gyi off to the remote Mong Sat Prison in eastern Shan State to serve a sixty-five-year, six-month prison sentence for participating in the same 2007 protest as Min Ko Naing. He was officially charged with breaking Burma's Electronics Act for issuing three political statements by email.

What everyone knew was that the arrest of both Ko Ko Gyi and Min Ko Naing was a preemptive strike by the regime to make sure that the student movement's top leaders were not free to coordinate the much bigger protests that were imminent, the Saffron Revolution. This may have been prescient by the regime, because some feel that if the two leaders had been involved, the uprising could have ended with a more positive result.

Ko Ko Gyi is greeted by supporters after his release
from prison (January 2012).

Ko Ko Gyi was born into a poor family in Rangoon's South Okkalapa
Township, just three months before General Ne Win's March 1962
military coup usurped Burma's nascent democratic government. He was
nicknamed "pickled salad" by his childhood friends because his mother
was a salad vendor. Though his mind was inclined towards philosophy and
art, at the behest of his father who worked in the timber industry he joined
a government technical school in Rangoon and later became a student at
Rangoon University, where he received a law diploma for his studies in
international relations and international administration.

Ko Ko Gyi's political life officially began in March 1988, when he
was in his final year studying at Rangoon University. Two RIT students
were killed during a police crackdown on a small campus protest, and
afterwards Ko Ko Gyi and some fellow students held a peaceful strike
on Rangoon University campus on March 15, 1988, to demand an official

investigation into the incident. Then, on Aug 8, 1988, Ko Ko Gyi went to Rangoon University, stood on a jeep, and gave a fifteen-minute speech emphasizing the importance of a democratic transition and demanding the official reestablishment of the banned student unions.

In early September 1988, U Nu announced the formation of an interim government, and Ko Ko Gyi promptly threw his support behind him, even traveling to Pegu Division to campaign. He was said to be indignant upon hearing that Suu Kyi did not support U Nu's bold move. Despite this criticism, it seemed that Ko Ko Gyi still supported Suu Kyi, and Tin Oo recalled a time around 1989 when he, Suu Kyi, and Ko Ko Gyi gave political speeches together. "I remember he was smart in articulating his views," said Tin Oo, adding that the NLD owes a debt of gratitude to the efforts of students like Ko Ko Gyi. "If it weren't for these students' activities, the NLD would not have come into existence,"[27] he said.

Ko Ko Gyi was arrested in 1991 for his involvement in the antigovernment protests at Rangoon University following the award of the Nobel Peace Prize to Suu Kyi. Sentenced to twenty years in jail, he was first held in Insein Prison in Rangoon and then in Thayet Prison in central Burma. During his incarceration, he spent some time in solitary confinement, but unlike Min Ko Naing was lucky, for the most part, to be able to mix with fellow inmates and to read and study smuggled books.

After his release from prison in 2005, Ko Ko Gyi picked up his political activities right where he had left off, and he and the charismatic Min Ko Naing formed the 88 Generation Students group (although by then they were both in their midforties). The group's activities—including its call for the public to directly send social justice complaints to the military chief, Senior General Than Shwe—reignited the opposition movement's political momentum that had slowed since Suu Kyi was placed under house arrest in 2003. "We are not afraid of being arrested again," Ko Ko Gyi said in September 2006. "We know how to survive in prison because we have spent fourteen to fifteen years behind bars. We are only worried that we cannot work for the people of Burma."[28]

Nervous about the wave of support building behind the 88 Generation Students group, the junta made sure that Ko Ko Gyi's concerns became a reality, and both he and Min Ko Naing found themselves behind bars once again in 2007. At least during his previous period of incarceration, Ko Ko Gyi was held in prisons close enough to home for his friends and family to visit him, but this time the Burmese authorities seemed determined to ensure that the student movement's leaders were as out of sight and silent as possible, and sent them to separate, remote prisons.

By isolating Ko Ko Gyi and limiting his contact with colleagues, the regime took away one of his main strengths. Fellow activists have said he is at his best in political strategy and discussions among small groups, because while he speaks slowly and clearly with sound argument, his slightly tense and subdued constitution and appearance make him a less powerful public speaker than his captivating and poetically inspired counterpart, Min Ko Naing.

In his own way, however, Ko Ko Gyi is a leader, as evidenced by his propensity to chart his own course rather than follow the crowd or conventional wisdom. For example, in contrast to many students who went into the jungles and took up arms against the regime in the aftermath of the failed 1988 uprising, Ko Ko Gyi stuck to his strong belief in finding solutions to the country's political deadlock by nonviolent means, although he told cellmates that he would support armed struggle if he felt it would lead to the desired political outcome. He also remained cautious about Suu Kyi's role in national politics, reminding others not to depend on one individual. He always told his colleagues that change would come from within, and he did not think international support and sanctions alone could bring about change to Burma, although he did not oppose sanctions in principle.

Since their release, the 88 Generation Students have continued to fight for democracy and have traveled extensively across Burma. They went to Kachin State to meet refugees who had fled from renewed fighting, and held meetings with politicians there. They also traveled to other ethnic states where they talked with ceasefire groups. This sent a positive signal that the former political prisoners could play a significant role in finding common ground in the struggle towards peace.

This conciliatory attitude does not, however, extend to all Burma's ethnic minoritites, notably the Rohingya. The Rohingya are a Muslim minority group within Burma that have long been denied citizenship, even though many of their families have lived in Burma for generations. The UN estimates that eight hundred thousand Rohingya live in Burma, where they face heavy-handed restrictions, needing government permission to marry, have more than two children, and travel outside of their villages. Human rights groups note that the widely reviled Rohingya are amongst the most persecuted people on Earth. In June 2012, soon after sectarian violence broke out in Arakan State between the Rohingya and the Buddhist Arakanese, Ko Ko Gyi was widely quoted as saying, "[The] Rohingya don't belong to ethnic groups in Burma . . . We won't accept any pressure from powerful nations . . . we will consider that they interfere in our country's affairs and sovereignty issues . . . If pressure continues we will consider this as a national issue and will join hand in hand with Burmese armed forces to solve [this problem]."[29] This is an opinion that reflects the contention between international human rights bodies and Burmese citizens. To most Burmese, however, the 88 Generation Students are thought of as attempting to build a bridge between ethnic divisions, particularly between the majority Burman and minority groups, as well as between the rebels and the Burmese government.

In August 2012, the 88 Generation Students commemorated the twenty-fourth anniversary of the 8888 uprising, and Min Ko Naing marked the occasion by making a speech in a video address:

Today is the day when we came out among the explosives and cheered our slogan. We were beaten by the butts of guns and batons on the street during our demonstration.

Sometimes when we walked down the street, our flag fell down when we were challenged. But we picked it up again and displayed it in the rain. We had to struggle very hard for the last twenty-four years.

Regarding national reconciliation, the president said that he wants all-inclusive politics. But there are our comrades who remain behind bars. There are also ethnic people who are behind bars for feeding one meal to the rebels. There should be no political prisoners.

Twenty-five years ago, the 88 Generation Students were on the streets fighting dictators. Yet, with the hope they held they also accepted bullets, blood, and tears. 1988 was the first time in modern Burmese history that an urban population and political forces united to oppose one-party rule. They were convinced that victory was imminent. They were all wrong. While some suspected that the armed forces may step in to restore order, few believed it would commit cold-blooded murder in broad daylight. The current reforms being implemented by the new regime are, doubtless, the long-awaited results of the 1988 uprising.

Min Ko Naing and Ko Ko Gyi are now in their early fifties, and while they have contributed immeasurably to the fight for democracy within Burma, they know that the struggle is not over yet. They also know that Suu Kyi, who is in her late sixties, as well as the other aged NLD leaders, cannot continue the struggle for democracy alone. There must be a new generation of visionary and dynamic leaders who can fill their roles in the movement. The question for the NLD and the 88 Generation Students is just who will do this? Who is this new generation that can continue in the fight to acheive a democratic Burma?

THE NEXT GENERATION

The junta knows that the support of Burma's youth is the NLD's driving force. And that worries them . . . That's why every effort of the NLD to mobilize its youth force is always followed by a junta campaign of repression.[30]

The NLD's youth members and Burma's young activists will soon form the backbone of the party and, understanding this, less than two months after her release from house arrest in 2010, Suu Kyi held a conference with NLD members, all of whom were under thirty-five years old, and many of whom had already been involved in social and humanitarian work. This was the first step in preparation for the social networking Suu Kyi intended to

NLD youths listen to a speech by Tin Oo at the youth conference held in December 2010.

do following her release. More than three hundred people attended the conference, which, to their surprise, went smoothly. Perhaps authorities did not intervene because it gave them a chance to easily identify the pool of young men and women that Suu Kyi believed were the future of her opposition political movement, as well as to appease the keenly observing Western governments.

Suu Kyi said in her opening speech,

> We are holding this meeting because the involvement of Burma's younger generations in the country's political, social, and economic affairs is essential . . . I would like to know how young people think and what is uppermost in their minds regarding how the country should progress.[31]

Suu Kyi added that she wanted to know where the opposition movement's weaknesses lay and how it should approach reform. Many of the young people in attendance had never seen the pro-democracy icon in person before the day of her release, let alone met her; some had not even been born when she gave her speech at Shwedagon Pagoda in 1988. Through their responses, Suu Kyi had the chance to learn the younger generation's point of view on Burma and their vision for the future.

Responses to the meeting were mixed. Many hoped to see a younger generation of activists playing a more prominent role in Burmese politics, but agreed with Suu Kyi that older leaders still have important contributions to make. One youth member was quoted as saying after the event, "I think these leaders should join hands with us and guide us . . . they should allow younger members to join with them because we now need strength for change."[32] There was also the hope that when Suu Kyi stated that she would like to create a peoples' network, that it could indicate a change from the present vertical hierarchy within the party toward a more horizontal approach, one that could reduce misunderstandings between the old and young political generations.

The disassociation that the youth members felt from the elderly uncles was also made clear. It was felt among many that the uncles had never had any social or political connection to the party's youth members or leaders, and that they had only met and begun to work together recently. While some youth members accepted that they often failed to appreciate the wisdom and experience of the old guard, they also believed that the elderly leaders were, at the same time, out of touch with the lifestyles and tastes of the new generation.

Taking this into account, and perhaps recognizing the divide in the party, in May 2012, in the wake of the April 1 by-elections, the NLD announced that it would hold a national conference during the last week of December, the first since since the party was formed in 1988. The conference aimed to democratically reform the NLD at every level throughout the country, with the nationwide central conference following lower-level regional conferences. And, although the uncles were to remain active within the party hierarchy as members of a "patrons committee." It seemed clear that the NLD was finally evolving.

At the top of the list of the things that Suu Kyi can learn from the NLD youth movement is the effective use of modern communication technology, new media, and social networking, which the Arab Spring events in the Middle East during early 2011 proved are critical to any well-organized effort to topple an authoritarian regime.

This will be a steep learning curve, as one of the major changes in the world during the time Suu Kyi was incarcerated was the emergence of new media on the Internet and the use of modern technology to broadcast breaking news and alternative ideas without having to resort to traditional media sources, which can be subject to censorship. The NLD's young members are technologically savvy and Facebook friendly, and although the numbers of Facebook users is small in Burma and among the exile community, interest in information technology has increased among young Burmese in recent years as access to the Internet in large cities like Rangoon, Mandalay, and Moulmein continues to grow.

Those that are familiar with the Internet have been able to use social networks to share information on Burmese politics. Through Gmail and G-talk, Skype and Facebook, networking inside and outside Burma is possible. Some even believe that Internet cafes in Rangoon and Mandalay will one day replace teashop-based Burmese civil society.

Unfortunately, the NLD, as led by its staunch elders, was exceedingly slow to adopt new media and modern technology as an effective tool while Suu Kyi was imprisoned. But, realizing its importance, immediately upon her release Suu Kyi expressed an interest in getting quickly up to speed on modern technology, and incorporating this modern communications technology into her opposition arsenal, saying she planned to use technology to build networks with the nation's ethnic minorities and supporters at home and abroad. This will take some doing, however, as until her release from house arrest Suu Kyi had never even spoken on a cell phone, much less blogged or tweeted. Reminding youth leaders of this, and after asking everyone in the audience to hold up their cell phones, Suu Kyi announced to those gathered at her NLD headquarters speech in 2010, "I used a phone like this for the first time yesterday. I did not even know where to talk into. Six years ago these did not exist here, now I see camera phones all over the place."[33] For most young Burmese Internet users, Suu Kyi's statement that she plans to use modern networking technology as a means of rebuilding the opposition movement was a welcome sign that she at least appreciates, if not yet completely understands, the modern world, despite her long years of isolation.

In a country such as Burma, the blossoming of the Internet has not, of course, passed unchecked. Following the 2007 Saffron Revolution, the military regime aggressively regulated social media, Internet forums, and e-mail. They also more strictly enforced the ownership of cyber cafés and required them to monitor users' screens and cooperate with criminal investigations. In addition, both online and offline censorship and information controls increased surrounding the November 7, 2010 national elections, with Internet connections interrupted between late October and the end of December that year.

In a report released in April 2011 by Washington-based information watchdog Freedom House, at that time Burma ranked second worst in the world for Internet freedom. The report said that the Burmese government aggressively regulated access to the Internet by its citizens and punished them for online activity that was seen as detrimental to the junta's security. According to the report, the military regime controlled Internet infrastructure in two ways, through total shutdowns and temporary reductions in bandwidth to slow the flow of information. Military sources inside Burma further confirmed this. The junta dispatched officers to Singapore, Russia, and powerhouse of censorship, North Korea for information-technology training, and these officers were assigned to monitor e-mail messages and telephone conversations, and to hack opposition websites. Between 2008 and 2011, many leading exile websites were temporarily shutdown by hackers through distributed denial-of-service (DDoS) attacks.

Over the past couple of years, however, it appears that the government has realized that it is an uphill battle to stem the use of the Internet in Burma, and since President Thein Sein assumed office there has been a great easing of restrictions on access to banned sites. Ever more, Burmese people are beginning to be able to access the Internet and discuss politics. This may be a double-edged sword, as generals have begun to use Burma's burgeoning social networks as a venue through which to spark racial tensions, most notably the anti-Muslim riots of 2012. The impact that this will have on the Burmese democracy movement remains to be seen.

THE SOCIAL ACTIVISTS

The spirit of Burma's 1988 uprising was not crushed during the crackdown on demonstrators, and neither was it confined to students and politicians. Many other heroes were discovered at that time and many more have been revealed over the last two decades under the repressive regime. Today, they continue to defy the junta in many ways. Some are famous and some work under the radar. They range from comedians and hip-hop musicians to health workers and human rights lawyers, but all contribute in their own way to Burma's struggle for democracy and human rights.

One of Burma's most famous social activists is Zarganar, a comedian who briefly spent time in prison after the 1988 uprising. He was known to have been roughly interrogated and there was speculation that the regime had used pliers to pull out his teeth, an excruciating form of torture. After his release in 1989, Zarganar appeared on stage and defiantly joked about his plight: "It's not true that my teeth were extracted . . . here they are!" he exclaimed, and then pulled a set of dentures from his mouth.[34]

The generals, however, were not laughing. A year later, Zarganar was rearrested and sentenced to five years in prison for impersonating General Saw Maung in front of thousands of fans. After his release he was banned from performing in public, but he could not stop making jokes at the expense of the humorless generals. Since he was not able to perform them himself, he turned to writing scripts for his fellow comedians, and eventually became a recipient of the Lillian Hellman and Dashiel Hammett Award, given by the Fund for Free Expression.

In 2008, however, Zarganar once again ended up on the wrong side of the junta, this time for speaking seriously about a serious matter. After traveling to the Irrawaddy Delta in the aftermath of Cyclone Nargis to assist in the relief effort, he was arrested for giving interviews to the BBC

Zarganar speaks at a press conference after returning from Arakan State (September 2012).

and *The Irrawaddy* about shortcomings in the regime's aid efforts and the slow response by UN agencies. He was later sentenced to forty-five years in prison for violating the Electronics Act, and a further fourteen years for offenses under four sections of the criminal code. In 2009, the Rangoon Division Court reduced Zarganar's prison term by twenty-four years, which still left him with a thirty-five-year sentence for speaking out on behalf of cyclone victims.

Zarganar was released in October 2011 with his quick wit still very much intact. When he flew to Bangkok for his first trip out of Burma to speak at the FCCT, he was not prepared to alter his performance, and voiced his realization at just how far behind Burma was in relation to its closest neighbor, Thailand. "When I saw the airplane I got a shock; when I saw the airport I got a shock; when I saw the big building and big bridge and good road I got a shock," he told a packed audience. The fifty year old also observed the faces of young people in Bangkok, adding that, unlike those in Burma, they expressed "freedom" and "self-confidence." "Our young people in my country, daily they worry . . . Their faces are full of anxieties," he said. "We are neighboring countries, but quite different." Zarganar is now enjoying his freedom and has also visited America, where he briefly met Secretary of State Hilary Clinton at the State Department. His message to her was that despite recent changes, Burma is not yet free.

Another celebrity, Kyaw Thu, is a famous actor and the founder of the Free Funeral Services Society. Established in 2001, the organization provides free funeral services to help shoulder the burden on the poor in coping with the cost of funerals, which have become increasingly expensive in Burma. The society assists by paying the cost of the transportation of the body to the cemetery, keeping the body at the mortuary, cremation, and glass or aluminum caskets. A benign, apolitical, and charitable activity, maybe, it was still not acceptable to the regime leaders, who regularly ordered local authorities to harass and intimidate the organization. Yet, Kyaw Thu has defied them and the service continues to grow, now handling between forty and eighty funerals a day in Rangoon. Kyaw Thu also played a prominent role in spearheading private relief efforts for victims of Cyclone Nargis, and opened a free clinic for the poor.

Also helping the cyclone victims was seventy-year-old Dr. Ashin Nyanissara, a respected abbot better known as Sitagu Sayadaw. His center, which he founded in 1980 and is known as the Sitagu International Buddhist Missionary Center, delivered relief items to the delta, rebuilt schools, and repaired over one thousand damaged monasteries. Sitagu Sayadaw stresses that compassion is the key aspect in whatever a person chooses to do. "If you lack compassion, you will be an irresponsible person,"[35] he warns. Practicing what he preaches, he has traveled extensively in Southeast Asia and raised funds to help people in need by giving talks on the dhamma.

Pho Phyu, also known as Yan Naing Aung, is a lawyer who helps farmers from different parts of Burma reclaim land that has been illegally confiscated. Many farmers do not receive sufficient agricultural loans from the government to be able to produce enough crops to cover their needs, so they end up borrowing from loan sharks who charge usurious rates of interest. The farmers cannot repay the loans even if they have a good yield, and are consequently forced to allow these loan sharks to grow rice on their land for a period of time. During that time, the lenders lay claim to the land with the local authorities and, as a result, many farmers end up being charged with trespassing for working on their own land, and stealing for harvesting their own yields. These loan sharks are, predictably, connected to those in power. "As far as we know there are powerful people, in terms of money or capital, behind those financiers," Pho Phyu said. "Farmers tell me that companies currently based in East Dagon Township are close to the authorities. They say that military personnel from the rank of major up to general are holding shares in those companies."[36]

Of course, as a lawyer opposing the activities of a government-sponsored criminal organization, Pho Phyu appeared on the government's radar. In 2009, he was arrested for helping farmers near Natmauk after a factory confiscated five thousand acres of farmland from farmers in the name of security and defense. After the confiscation, farmers had to rent their own land from the new "owner," and were forced to grow castor-oil plants for the factory. When a local resident who reported this to the International Labour Organization (ILO) was charged with leaking government secrets, Pho Phyu defended him in court and also filed land cases. To stop Pho Phyu from participating in the trial, the authorities detained him. Unable to find any offense, they declared that his legal team was illegal and charged him under the Unlawful Association Act. He was sentenced to four years imprisonment, but the ILO intervened and he was released after fourteen months.[37]

Undeterred by his imprisonment, Pho Phyu recently represented fishermen and their families after thousands were swept out to sea in a tropical storm in March 2010. In addition, he is currently assisting farmers to reclaim more than ten thousand acres in Rangoon and about two thousand acres in Irrawaddy Division. When asked why he continued to persevere in the face of such personal danger, Pho Phyu simply replied, "They are starving right in front of my eyes. That's why I am working for them."[38]

Pho Phyu is not the only human rights lawyer risking his life to help land confiscation victims. Another lawyer, Aye Myint, set up a legal aid group called Guiding Star to handle cases of forced labor, illegal land-confiscation, and workers' rights, and as a result was awarded the European Bar's Ludovic-Trarieux Thirteenth International Human Rights Prize in 2008 for his work under repressive conditions. Aye Myint was sentenced to life imprisonment in 2003 for his connections with the ILO and the Federation of Trade Unions (Burma) in exile, but after the ILO's intervention the sentence was reduced to three years. Since his release from this sentence, Aye Myint has been jailed many times and his lawyer's license has been seized by the authorities, but he continues to take on human rights cases. "The struggle for justice will continue," he said in an interview with DVB. "I want the oppressed in Burma to know that our victory will come soon. . . . I also want the military regime to know that we won't accept any unjust government."[39]

Phyu Phyu Thin is an NLD youth leader who has been involved in helping HIV/AIDS patients since 2002. Her NLD-affiliated welfare group runs three shelters in Rangoon that house around one hundred HIV/AIDS patients and provides food, bedding, antiretroviral treatment, and other medication. "When we [the NLD] initiated the HIV/AIDS project, we only intended to educate patients and the public about the risks of HIV/AIDS, but once we saw the needs of the victims we realized we had to take care of them,"[40] said Phyu Phyu Thin, adding that patients come to the shelters because they trust the clinics and feel that the staff do not discriminate against them.

Suu Kyi visited the hospice soon after her release, and shortly afterwards The New Light of Myanmar reported that the HIV/AIDS shelters would be closed because of the "possible spread of infectious disease from the patients,"[41] citing government health officials. Afterwards, HIV/AIDS patients living at one of the shelters stated that none of them wanted to relocate because they did not believe that the assistance provided at the new location would be as good as that provided by Phyu Phyu Thin with the support of Suu Kyi. "If the patients don't want to move, we will stand in front of them even if authorities try to arrest us,"[42] said Phyu Phyu Thin, who defied the order and continued her work. Other prominent female activists include Nilar Thein, Su Su Nway, Naw Ohn Hla, and ZinMar Aung, who have also been persecuted for their work.

Burma's youth is also rising to the challenge and following the lead of their activist elders. In 2000, hip-hop singer Zayar Thaw and his band Acid released the first ever hip-hop album in Burma and it went straight to number one. Since then, Zayar Thaw has used his music and popularity to raise awareness and funds by performing in charity concerts, such as one in which he teamed up with two famous Burmese poets, Saw Wai and currently exiled Aung Way, for a fundraising event for HIV orphans sponsored by a charity founded by Zarganar.

Following the violent suppression of the 2007 demonstrations, Zayar Thaw and other artists used hip-hop and rap to air their political views and satirize the regime. He then joined a number of young activists in forming a group called Generation Wave that secretly recorded and distributed antigovernment music, as well as leaflets and stickers. As a result, Generation Wave was soon placed on the regime's blacklist and Zayar Thaw was arrested along with several colleagues. In 2008, minutes before he was sentenced to six years in prison on charges of membership in an illegal organization, the young hip-hop artist wrote a statement that was leaked out to Generation Wave members, saying, "Tell the people to have the courage to reject the things they don't like, and even if they don't dare to openly support the right thing, tell them not to support the wrong thing."[43]

The arrest of Zayar Thaw and his colleagues failed to break up Generation Wave, and the remaining members of the group continued to produce secret recordings, often in makeshift studios constructed in members' homes. One of the numbers on a 2009 CD issued to commemorate the second anniversary of the 2007 demonstrations, is titled "Wake Up!" and appeals to young people to join in the pro-democracy movement. Another number, "Please Excuse Me," is a request for a mother's permission to join the opposition struggle. "At first, I feared being an activist, but by being one I overcame that fear," said one Generation Wave artist, COT.[44]

To distribute their clandestine recordings, Generation Wave members secretly dropped CDs at teashops. The group also had a website from which its albums and singles could be downloaded, and the Burmese services of the BBC, VOA, Radio Free Asia, and DVB have all broadcast Generation Wave music.

Generation Wave received a shot of adrenalin in May 2011 when Zayar Thaw was released from prison. With several of his colleagues still behind bars, he was determined to continue using his talents to help the people of Burma and to speak out on behalf of freedom and democracy. But in August 2011, he was told by local authorities that if he performed at an upcoming charity concert the event would be cancelled.[45] This prompted Zayar Thaw to say, "The government has declared that it is a democratic government, so it has the responsibility to explain who has imposed a ban on me, and why."[46] The young hip-hop singer joined the NLD before the April 1, 2012 by-elections and won a parliamentary seat for a constituency in the government stronghold of Naypyidaw. He was only in his thirties, but could discuss the need for national reconciliation, as well as the plight of the ethnic minorities.

A Burmese blogger, Nay Phone Latt, joined Burma's online resistance movement but was arrested in 2008 and sentenced to twenty years in prison for blogging about the regime's brutal crackdown on the Saffron Revolution. Released in January 2012 under the presidential amnesty, the thirty-two year old once again threw himself into the online resistance movement through social media, and has become a poster boy for opposition to the former junta. While in detention, he won the PEN/Barbara Goldsmith Freedom to Write Award in New York for showing "strength of the creative spirit" in the face of repression. He remains one of the forces of the online resistance movement in Burma; the junta's fear of which represents the importance of the dissemination of information, both to those within Burma and out to the international community.

THE MEDIA

If I do wrong, write about me. If the queens do wrong, write about them. If my sons and my daughters do wrong, write about them. If the judges and mayors do wrong, write about them. No one shall

take action against the journals for writing the truth. They shall go
in and out of the palace freely.

King Mindon, the penultimate king of Burma (r. 1853–78) understood the
value of a free press and, with these words, formed Burma's first indigenous
press freedom law, giving Burma one of the freest presses in Southeast
Asia. During British colonialism, the media was used to spread nationalist
sentiment, and journals rallied behind the independence movement, giving
national icons such as Aung San a venue for the spread of their ideas as
they were published in Burma's two renowned newspapers, *The Sun* and
The New Light of Burma. Despite the strictures of British rule, throughout
the decades there was a steady increase in the number of periodicals and
newspapers in circulation, from forty-four publications in 1911 to 103
in 1921, and more than two hundred by the 1930s. Between Burmese
independence in 1948, and 1962, when General Ne Win seized power, the
country experienced one of the liveliest media environments in Asia, with
press freedom further enshrined by the 1947 constitution.

Unfortunately, this writers' paradise was not set to last and, until
recently, press freedom had deteriorated steadily to the point that in May
2010, Senior General Than Shwe was named in the top forty of the annual
Reporters Without Borders list of world "Predators of Press Freedom,"
alongside such figures as North Korean despot Kim Jong-il, Zimbabwe's
Robert Mugabe, and Saudi Arabian Prime Minister Abdullah ibn Abdulaziz
Al-Saud. At the same time, for several consecutive years Reporters Without
Borders ranked Burma among the world's five worst countries for press
freedom. Recently, as Burma slowly opens to the world, press freedom
has once again made it onto the agenda, and with the abolition of the
censorship board the country has begun to show marked loosening of
the strictures on the press.

Burma's descent from relative freedom to absolute censorship and
back began shortly after the March 1962 coup, when journalists formed
the Burma Press Council in response to fears of a junta crackdown. Their
fears were well founded. Foreign news agencies were soon evicted from
the country and newspapers were often either closed completely, resulting
in the lengthy imprisonment of many journalists, or they were nationalized.

The new strictures extended to all forms of publishing, including novels, news, short stories, cartoons, and drawings, which were all made to go through the censorship board, despite reassurances by the government that full freedom of expression was, in fact, permitted within the accepted limits of the "Burmese Way to Socialism."

Government controls were briefly lifted during the popular uprising in 1988, forming a small burst of freedom as several publications were able to be published without going through the censorship board. Inevitably, however, with the crackdown on protesters came a crackdown on the media, and this mini-rennaissance was tragically short-lived. The years that followed the 1988 uprising, a time when Suu Kyi and many of her colleagues were behind bars, were characterized by strict control of the press by the ruling junta, and many journalists imprisoned, intimidated, or forced from reporting the news. For the next two decades, Burma would become a haven of both official censorship and bullied self-censorship.

By election day in 2010, only twenty-five Burmese journalists working for foreign news agencies were allowed to cover the polls, along with two Chinese correspondents. A Japanese journalist who attempted to slip across the border was arrested in Myawaddy, opposite the Thai town of Mae Sot, while several local reporters were briefly detained and interrogated. The release of Suu Kyi less than a week after the elections, however, caught the imagination of Burmese and foreigners alike. Foreign journalists found ways to enter the country on tourist visas and flocked to Suu Kyi's lakeside home, as did local reporters eager for an interview and the opportunity to push the censorship envelope.

As expected, following Suu Kyi's release there was no reaction from the regime other than a report the following day in the state-run newspaper *The New Light of Myanmar* saying that Suu Kyi had been pardoned because of good behavior during her years of house detention. Independent journals did test the waters, but quickly found that Suu Kyi's freedom was by no means the beginning of new press freedoms in Burma, as the censorship board, known as the Press Scrutiny and Registration Division (PSRD), which exercised draconian controls over news reporting, ordered the domestic media to carry limited news about the pro-democracy icon, and forbade them from printing any large pictures of Suu Kyi, or from putting any images of Suu Kyi on their front pages. In terms of content, only "positive" comments from Suu Kyi's first speech were permitted for publication, and the media could not mention the fact that NLD would focus on political activities.

Despite the regime's efforts to restrict news about Suu Kyi, most news journals still could not resist the chance to boost their sales by testing the PSRD's limits in their coverage of her release. "Most journals printed it as a supplement. When they sold the copies on the bookshelves, this supplement with a large photo of Suu Kyi became the cover. Of course, they are now sold out,"[47] a Rangoon-based editor explained.

Other publications used ingenius methods to skirt the draconian censorship laws, and one in particular, the leading sports journal First Eleven, used a clever combination of headlines about English Premier League match results to splash news of Suu Kyi's release on its front page. By playing with the colors and placement of the letters of a seemingly innocent headline, the journal was able to spell out the message, "Su Free Unite & Advance to Grab The Hope." A proofreader at the PSRD told The Irrawaddy, "The copy we read was in black and white. We were not aware of it. When the publication was released, people quickly began talking about it. After that, the Ministry of Information took action against the journal."[48]

Once the excitement of Suu Kyi's initial reappearance on the national political stage had died down, Burmese journalists were faced with a different predicament. Parliament convened for the first time in twenty-two years on January 31, 2011, but during the first session reporters were not allowed anywhere near the new parliament buildings in Naypyidaw. Those who tried were removed and returned empty-handed. The censorship board reasserted its power over the local journals and, in response to their activities over the previous months, then suspended publication of First Eleven and the Hot News Journal for two weeks, while other journals such as 7 Days News, The Voice, Venus News, Pyithu Khit, Myanmar Post, The Snap Shot, and Myanmar Newsweek were suspended for one week. The PSRD, headed by ex-Major Tint Swe, said the two-week suspensions were for including information that it had not approved, while one-week suspensions were given to journals covering the Suu Kyi news with an extra full-page report, or using more than one photo.

In addition to the suspensions, a week after the release of Suu Kyi the PSRD called an emergency meeting with journal editors. Sources said the meeting lasted three hours and was more of a berating than a discussion. Tint Swe, who also writes propaganda articles under the pen name of Yeyint Tint Swe, told editors he did not want the journals to cut Suu Kyi news totally, but warned that "great editors" must be careful. The PSRD later sent the editors of journals a list of ten rules, and the sanctions they would incur for not respecting them. The penalties included the confiscation of printed material, temporary or permanent suspension of publishing rights, confiscation of printing presses, and lengthy prison sentences under laws first introduced in 1962 when the military seized power.

Shortly afterwards, reporters working inside Burma were sent a clear message that testing these limits and defying the regime could indeed earn them lengthy prison sentences. In February 2011, photojournalist Maung Maung Zeya received a thirteen-year sentence for filming the scene of bomb blasts in Rangoon in 2010. He joined some dozen other journalists in Burma's prisons, including his son Sithu Zeya who was arrested in connection with the same incident, and Hla Hla Win, a broadcast journalist sentenced to twenty years in prison for violating the vague and draconian Electronics Act, which remains the single biggest concern of reporters and commentators in Burma. All three journalists reportedly worked for the DVB exile news agency based in Oslo, Norway, and were all freed in the January 2012 amnesty.

Small slivers of media freedom seemed to begin after Thein Sein made a passing reference to the role of the media in his first address to his cabinet. After he was sworn in as president in April 2011, Thein Sein regularly mentioned the importance of the "fourth pillar," the media, in his national speeches or in interviews to foreign media. This alone was unusual in Burma since many military leaders were either shy or they hated speaking to the press, particularly the foreign press, as they were often seen as enemies of the state. Since that time, media observers began to notice differences in the level of censorship in private journals.

The loosening of the strictures hinted at by Thein Sein was noticed almost immediately. Shortly after his inaugeration, readers of the *Weekly Eleven* were pleasantly surprised to see a picture of Aung San Suu Kyi in a supplement affixed to an article about a ceremony marking the tenth anniversary of the Free Funeral Services Society. It was the first time that Suu Kyi's picture had appeared in a local journal in the five months since journals were suspended for their "excessive coverage" of her release from house arrest the previous November. The article did not, however, mention her by name.

On June 10, 2011, Burma's Ministry of Information confirmed that it was relaxing its censorship of the country's media, and conditionally changed censorship regulations from a "precensorship" to a "postcensorship" mode on five topics: sports, entertainment, technology, health, and children's literature. In addition, in past years the PSRD cut issues such as deforestation, illegal logging, wildlife trading, and the negative impact of hydropower projects because they were thought to be too sensitive to publish. Afterwards, however, there was some small space to discuss these issues.

Despite these changes, the PSRD still remained at the helm, and although it had instructions to allow articles on the five nonpolitical issues to go directly to print, it had the authority, and actively continued, to monitor those articles after they had been published. Publishers themselves were also warned to adhere to the three national causes—nondisintegration of the Union, nondisintegration of national solidarity, and perpetuation of sovereignty—and avoid printing anything that could destabilize the state. It appeared that the apparent relaxation of regulations by the PSRD was deceptive, and that publishers were, in effect, being warned to practice self-censorship. Furthermore, with the exceptions of sports, entertainment, health, technology, and children's literature, other topics—such as politics, economy, and crime—still had to pass through the PSRD's red pens before they could go to press. The editors of all weekly journals, monthly magazines, and books in Burma still had to submit their proposed drafts to the Burmese censorship board ahead of publication, and political reports and critical opinion pieces remained off limits.

In addition, aside from news about Suu Kyi's movements, there were other issues that remained very much taboo for Burmese reporters. Human rights violations that remained rife in conflict zones, especially in eastern Burma, went unreported. No Burmese publication would dared have hinted of the rape, murder, and forced relocation that were part of the Burmese army's campaign to impose its will on ethnic minorities. Even the impact of megaprojects that would transform Burma's landscape forever, affecting millions of its citizens, were not discussed within the pages of the country's newspapers. Furthermore, coverage of the endemic nepotism and cronyism among the military elite and their families, far less reports about how generals' families embezzled state assets, remained muted.

Despite the ever-present list of restrictions, there were further signs of encouragement for the Burmese media in August 2011, when all of Burma's major journals carried pictures of Suu Kyi's face-to-face meeting with Thein Sein in Naypyidaw. One veteran journalist stated, "The meeting between Daw Aung San Suu Kyi and the president is an indisputable fact. Therefore, journals reported it because it was directly concerned with the president. Given some extent of freedom to report this event, we are now enjoying somewhat more freedom of expression than before." But while Suu Kyi's visit to Naypyidaw made splash headlines in private journals, the county's state-run press only reported it in brief. "There could be some underlying reasons why government newspapers reported it so briefly," the veteran journalist continued. "At present, we cannot say precisely to what extent we will continue to enjoy such freedom from censorship."[49]

A year later, in August 2012, the Ministry of Information stated that it had ended all precensorship. However, the government still monitors news and bulletins, and the censorship board has not yet been abolished. In addition, Burma's 1962 Printers and Publishers Registration Act, which was imposed shortly after General Ne Win seized power, is still in place. Moreover, editorial staff at journals are still required to follow sixteen guidelines towards protecting the three national causes, as well as "journalistic ethics," to ensure their stories are accurate and do not jeopardize national security.

In September 2012, Thein Sein reshuffled his cabinet and replaced Kyaw

Hsan with the more moderate Aung Kyi, who immediately announced that Burma would allow daily newspapers by 2013. Aung Kyi said he was aware of several problems under Kyaw Hsan, including the key issue of censorship, and was quoted as saying by *The Myanmar Times*, "It is my sincere belief that daily [private sector] newspapers are essential for a democratic country." Even the state-run newspapers then began to relax, reporting Suu Kyi's speeches given during her trips abroad and her visits to Western countries, although they still practice self-censorship. The government still controls publishing licenses, and several leading publications in Burma are either close to the regime or are owned by family members of regime leaders. There is little incentive to publish incendiary or sensitive issues such as large-scale corruption cases involving former or current military dictators or leaders; inside stories into military affairs; and criticism and opinion-based editorials toward state and government leaders.

Promises on Burmese media freedom have occurred frequently in recent years, and they have always come with conditions that effectively nullify their value. Only time will tell if these most recent assurances hold any more weight than their counterparts in previous years.

ETHNIC GROUPS

After the country regained its independence from the British in 1948, Burma plunged almost immediately into civil war. The country faced a multifaceted insurgency from communists and a number of different groups of ethnic rebels. Comprising one-third of the population in Burma, ethnic minorities asked for equal rights to preserve their culture, language, and identity, and for their Panglong Agreement rights that guaranteed them autonomy within a federal state. They had been persecuted, exploited, and discriminated against, and they asked to share resources equally. Since 1948, although there is no official figure, it is estimated that hundreds of thousands of lives have been lost in their fight for equality.

Under Ne Win the civil war widened, and the government implemented a counterinsurgency campaign in the states where armed ethnic groups were operating. In doing so, the regime implemented the infamous "four cuts" strategy, in which they attempted to cut off food, finance, intelligence, and recruits from the armed ethnic groups. Until 1988, Burma's urban population and student activists were cut off from the ethnic struggle and did not really empathize with it or comprehend the deeply rooted issues driving the civil war. The 1988 uprising, however, created a link between the urban political movement and the jungle-based insurgencies when thousands of student activists fled the cities to hide in the areas controlled by ethnic insurgents. However, while the urban groups and the ethnic groups had better communication and a better understanding of each other's struggle, there remained a long way to go for true reconciliation between groups who appeared to be fighting for the same side.

Prior to 1989, although the regime waged war against communists and ethnic militias for decades, any efforts at negotiating a ceasefire always broke down when the regime insisted that the insurgents surrender their weapons. In 1989, however, the Communist Party of Burma (CPB) faced

ABSDF (All Burma Students Democratic Front) fighters in a KNU/KNLA-controlled area (2000). The author is in the center. Courtesy Nic Dunlop

an internal mutiny, lost the support of China, and suddenly collapsed. Following this, the new regime reached a ceasefire with the ethnic Wa and Kokang who had rebelled inside the CPB, and as a result the regime turned a blind eye to the lucrative business of opium production and drug trafficking in those regions. Then, in 1995, like a house of cards falling, the ethnic Kachin, Mon, and Shan all entered ceasefire agreements with the junta.

The problem for the next fifteen years was that a ceasefire was a short-term cure rather than a long-term solution; it was not sustainable, and eventually the underlying problem needed to be treated. As a result, for a decade and a half after the agreements were signed, the ethnic situation remained tense. The ethnic leaders still did not trust the regime, or for that matter the Burmese ethnic majority as a whole, and the generals did not want to recognize the ethnic groups or grant them any form of real autonomy.

In April 2009, the regime proposed that armed ethnic ceasefire groups would be transformed into members of a border guard force (BGF) that would be under government military command. This proposal met strong resistance from nearly all ethnic militias, who were unwilling to reduce the current pseud-autonomy they enjoyed or surrender their arms, which they saw as essential to their ability to resist total government control over their ethnic regions. The regime leaders simply did not understand the struggle of the rebel groups. In the end, what the ethnic groups wanted was total autonomy over the regions where their people live, while the regime wanted to grant minimal, if any, representation.

The BGF proposal turned out to be one of the Than Shwe regime's biggest blunders, and tensions between the junta and ceasefire groups rose steadily, concurrent with the approach of the 2010 election, as the generals attempted to use the impending polls to pressure the armed militias to join the BGF. When several ethnic armies officially rejected the BGF proposal, the already deep-seated mistrust grew, and fears grew that a breakdown of the ceasefire was imminent.

Major ceasefire groups like the Kachin Independence Army (KIA) and the United Wa State Army (UWSA) began recruiting more foot soldiers, buying more weapons, and preparing for military mobilization and guerilla warfare in case armed conflict broke out. They also acquired antiaircraft weapons and additional ammunition, and deployed their troops along key hilltop positions. In addition, they formed an alliance with four other armed ethnic groups, the Karen, Mon, Karenni, and Chin, although deep skepticism remained on the legitimacy of the alliance, as previous ethnic alliances had always been symbolic gestures that did not translate into action.[50]

Soon after the election that propelled Thein Sein into power, several ethnic groups took advantage of the newfound political opening, and a domino effect of ceasefires and opportunities sprung up. The ethnic groups benefited in the same way as urban-based opposition groups and activists by establishing contacts and exchanging views. However, the political opening has not brought peace or stability to the troubled regions, and the new government's success in calming the conflict, so far, has seemed limited.

Soldiers in front-line positions under fire at Hkaya Bum outpost, Kachin State, which the Burmese armed forces tried unsuccessfully to capture for over a week. The soldier in the foreground holds a captured Burmese army assault rifle (January 2013). Courtesy Steve Tickner

The biggest prize the Thein Sein administration has won since his election is an informal ceasefire agreement with the main ethnic group of the Karen National Union (KNU), after sixty-three years of conflict. In April 2011, KNU delegations went to meet the president in Naypyidaw, and KNU General-Secretary Naw Zipporah Sein and Thein Sein agreed to the ceasefire.

Thein Sein, who once led troops on the frontline, understands how badly Burma needs peace. However, in reality, a nationwide ceasefire remains unrealistic. There remain lingering questions on the *Tatmadaw*'s willingness to end the conflicts and embrace peace, and the president does not seem to have the requisite authority to order a genuine end to the killing.

Major Sai Lao Hseng, the main spokesperson for the Shan State Army–South (SSA–South), which signed a ceasefire with the government in December 2011, stated that Naypyidaw is responsible for implementing the truce by directing its troops on the ground. He said, "We agreed that the end of ethnic conflict is the key in peace-building. That's why we accepted the government's offer of the ceasefire." "The government wanted to start with a ceasefire. So we signed it. But the ceasefire is just an agreement on paper. We think it doesn't yet reflect the reality."[51] In Shan State, despite the agreement, skirmishes are reported on a regular basis.

Beyond Shan State, fighting continues in Karenni and Karen States, and, most notably, in Kachin State where the human cost of the conflict is being felt most acutely. Peace in Kachin State remains a distant dream. Hundreds of people have so far lost their lives, thousands have been maimed or injured, and at least seventy thousand have been displaced from their homes. The conflict between the Kachin rebels and Burmese armed forces shows no sign of abating and the refugee crisis is worsening. Kachin rebel leaders accuse the Burmese military generals of ignoring government-initiated reforms, as conflicts on the ground continue.

Aung Min, Burma's chief peace negotiator and a powerful minister attached to the President's Office, attempted to reach out to the Kachin in late 2012, but the conflict continued to escalate and casualties were frequent. Like the democratic transition in Burma, the peace process remains fragile, and the government must not forget that the root of its problems has always been its failure to address the political needs and aspirations of its ethnic peoples. Until these needs are fulfilled and the armed forces are called back to the barracks, the bloodshed will continue.

To most ethnic groups, a ceasefire is simply the initial step that should eventually lead to a dialogue to address key social, economic, and political issues. It is not an ultimate solution and ethnic leaders are unlikely to accept Naypyidaw imperialism. Ethnic groups also treat the motives behind the government's olive branch with deep suspicion, as many mega-projects are being developed in Karen, Shan, Mon, Kachin, and Arakan States that put local people at risk of exploitation. They believe that the latest peace initiatives are being driven by the desire for economic development in their regions and external business incentives, rather than a desire for national reconciliation.

Thein Sein has done little to allay these suspicions. When addressing a union-level peace committee in early 2012, he said, "The transition should lead in a political and economic direction as this is the foundation of the country," adding that a failure to end the war in ethnic areas would be an obstacle to economic development, and that the continued presence of armed ethnic groups in the country weakens the rule of law in building a democratic process. The rule of law may be important, but the underlying problem is that the ethnic groups feel they are being treated as second-class citizens. In addition, economic development and mega-projects will not bring prosperity to minority regions and end ethnic conflicts.

The Burmese people, including the ethnic leaders, are looking to Suu Kyi to provide leadership with respect to reconciliation. She is well aware that she is expected to be at the forefront of any push to bring all the disparate groups together and find common ground. When meeting with veteran politicians shortly after her release, Suu Kyi said that fostering a "Panglong spirit" is needed in the effort to achieve national reconciliation, an opinion matched by both armed ethnic ceasefire and nonceasefire groups, who mostly support a second Panglong Conference.[52]

Pu Cin Sian Thang, a spokesman for the United Nationalities Alliance, a group consisting of ethnic representatives who were elected in 1990 but

A shocked mother and her two-year-old son recover in Laiza hospital in January 2013, after both were injured in the Burmese army's artillery attack on central Laiza, Kachin State, which killed three civilians. The attack was denied by the Burmese goverment. Courtesy Steve Tickner

never allowed to claim their seats in parliament, said that ethnic leaders and the public trust Suu Kyi and believe she is the best person to lead a second Panglong Conference. "I believe she has accepted this duty for the sake of the country's future, even though there are many dangers she could face. It shows how much she is willing to sacrifice for us. The Panglong spirit means equality for all ethnic groups," Pu Cin Sian Thang said.[53] However, he said that backing such a conference would be a big challenge that carries real risks for her, including detention by the junta. For that reason, he said, Suu Kyi should consider inviting the military as one of the stakeholders in the planned conference.[54] Emphasizing this, in its first official response to calls by Suu Kyi and others for talks to address Burma's ethnic divisions and achieve national reconciliation, the country's state-run media warned that moving ahead with a conference without the backing of the military risked putting the opposition on a collision course with the ruling regime, stating that the proposed ethnic conference "would go against the junta's current seven-step political road map."[55] The article continued, "Parliament is the best place to strengthen the already gained national unity. . . . If they [the opposition] choose to follow this idealistic way while ignoring the best way [parliament], they should be aware that that it will bring more harm than good to the country."[56] The article also warned that without the *Tatmadaw*, a conference like the Panglong Conference would be manipulated by organizations that oppose the government and its seven-step political road map, even if it is carried out with goodwill.[57] Ethnic leaders themselves, however, denied that they were trying to exclude the Burmese military from the process. "The Panglong spirit is about achieving national unity, and this can't be done without the *Tatmadaw*," said Pu Cin Sian Thang.[58]

As the regime suggested, Suu Kyi, opposition members, and ethnic groups began gently trying to raise the sensitive issue of Burma's ethnic minorities in parliament. In August 2012, in her first speech to the legislature, Suu Kyi called for laws protecting the rights of the country's impoverished ethnic minorities and an end to discrimination as part of the "emergence of a genuine democratic country."[59] She elaborated, saying, "To become a truly democratic union, with a spirit of the union, equal rights, and mutual respect, I urge all members of parliament to discuss the enactment of the laws needed to protect equal rights of ethnicities."[60]

Suu Kyi's comments came in support of a motion by an ethnic Shan MP from the ruling USDP on upholding ethnic minority rights. She also pointed out soaring poverty rates in Chin, Kachin, Shan, and Arakan States, noting that protecting minority rights required more than just maintaining ethnic languages and cultures. "The high poverty rates in ethnic states clearly indicate that development in ethnic regions is not satisfactory— and ethnic conflicts in these regions have not ceased,"[61] she said during the brief speech.

Thein Sein's government's belated approach to reconciliation may be due to a realization that without a solution to the ethnic issues there can be no political transition in Burma. Unless the underlying causes of the war are addressed, the days of armed conflict on multiple fronts in Burma may return and any hopes for national reconciliation could be destroyed.

THE SANGHA

Throughout Burmese history, the community of Buddhist monks has played a pivotal role at nearly every political turning point. Today, the sangha, (the sons of Buddha) is the biggest institution in Burma after the armed forces. They are in close contact with the common people, and witness firsthand the suffering and poverty of ordinary Burmese citizens. Because of this, they have a very clear picture of the situation in the country and, arguably, have a more complete network, more connections, and a greater influence than politically active students, who have been constantly watched, imprisoned, or forced into exile.

When General Ne Win overthrew U Nu's government in the 1962 military coup, he began immediately to sow seeds of resistance within Burma's clergy. The new regime chief regarded monks as potential opposition and, once he had acheived power, he developed a strategy of issuing identity cards to members of the sangha in order to control them. The monastic community was unimpressed, and both senior abbots and young monks refused to attend a meeting held in the mid-1960's to implement the strategy.

This tension between Ne Win's regime and the sangha remained throughout his tenure, and in 1980 he launched a carefully orchestrated effort to discredit the monastic community known as the "sangha reform" campaign, with the supposed aim of "cleaning up the sangha." Far from its superficial aim, the campaign was, in fact, a smear campaign used to justify a crackdown on the monastic order. Before the campaign, intelligence officers and government informants infiltrated temples disguised as monks and gathered information about monks and abbots. Well-known abbots including Thein Phyu Sayadaw, Mahasi Sayadaw, and Burma's top Buddhist scholar, Tipitaka Mingun Sayadaw, were targeted in the campaign for their refusal to cooperate with Ne Win's government.

Following this, Ne Win established a State Sangha Maha Nayaka Committee, which, due to generous financial backing, actually received some recognition from elderly Buddhists and was approached by the Burmese government to help quell the 1988 uprising. Senior monks appeared in live television broadcasts appealing to the public for calm. Then, in August 1988, just days after the 8888 uprising and subsequent massacre in Rangoon, monks expressed sorrow for the loss of life and also—to the surprise of many—appealed to the regime to govern in accordance with Buddhism's ten duties prescribed for rulers of the people. The appeal failed to calm the public mood, but the people did recognize that the monks were entreating the regime leaders to be good rulers, and during the uprising many temples offered to harbor activists who had gone into hiding from the intelligence authorities. In addition, as the extent of the violence became known to all, some members of the sangha showed even more overt signs of support for the protesters. On August 30, the *Working People's Daily* reported that fifteen hundred monks had marched in a procession through the Rangoon streets and gathered in front of the Rangoon General Hospital emergency ward, where they recited *Metta Sutta* in memory of monks, workers, and students who were dying in the struggle for democracy.[62]

Following the military coup in 1988, confrontations between rebellious monks and the authorities continued. In 1990, government troops in Mandalay fired on the crowds, killing several people including monks. Angered by the military's brutality, Mandalay monks began a *patta ni kozana kan,* refusing to accept alms from members of the armed forces and their families. The brutality continued. In one incident, the Mandalay Division commander at the time, Major General Tun Kyi, invited senior monks and abbots to attend a religious ceremony, but not one person came. Military leaders then realized the seriousness of the boycott and decided to launch a crackdown.[63] In Mandalay alone, more than 130 monasteries were raided, and monks were defrocked and imprisoned. Nationwide, as many as three hundred monks and at least nine respected senior abbots were defrocked and arrested, including the highly respected Thu Mingala, a Buddhist literature laureate who was sentenced to eight years in prison.[64]

The 1990 crackdown divided the sangha community. The late Mingun Sayadaw, who was secretary of the State Sangha Maha Nayaka Committee, was ridiculed by young monks for not supporting the boycott campaign, and in their minds for allying himself with the junta. Some referred to him as "Senior General Mingun Sayadaw," and when he visited one temple in Mandalay young monks reportedly saluted him.

The generals have, of course, not wanted to see Suu Kyi develop too close a relationship with the influential sangha, and they have applied divide and rule strategies in attempts to keep the monks and the opposition leaders separate. In 1996, for example, the regime accused the NLD of infiltrating the sangha in order to plan and commit subversive acts against the authorities. In addition, the junta has attempted to openly and audaciously bribe the sangha. Aside from holding numerous merit-making ceremonies and offering valuable gifts to monks, military leaders launched well-publicized pagoda restoration projects throughout Burma. In one spectacular bid to win the hearts and minds of the sangha, the generals borrowed a Buddha tooth relic from China and toured the country with it, and also held a World Buddhist Summit. Then, in 1999, military leaders renovated Shwedagon Pagoda after the *htidaw*, the sacred umbrella, was removed amid reports of minor local earthquakes. Restoration of the pagoda complex, however, did nothing to help the generals' image. Many Burmese found it hard to believe their military leaders' claims that they were actually preserving Buddhism, which certainly did not permit the military to beat, defrock, imprison, and kill monks. In any case, the generals and their families seemed to place more trust in astrology and numerology than in Buddhist ritual. They treasured white elephants and lucky charms, and were constantly seeking advice from astrologers. Even when the generals were building pagodas and erecting Buddha images, the projects were based on astrological predictions and readings.

In contrast to the generals, Suu Kyi has taken a successfully nonsuperstitious path to establishing a relationship with the sangha that goes back to her first days as a national leader. When Suu Kyi entered Burmese politics in 1988, she made a campaign tour around the country that included visits to numerous temples and meetings with monks and abbots, and after being released from house arrest in 1995, she traveled to Karen State to meet Bhaddanta Vinaya—then Burma's most respected monk—who was better known as Thamanya Sayadaw. Like Suu Kyi, Thamanya Sayadaw was revered not only for his humanitarian work, but also for his refusal to kowtow to the regime leaders. He had been approached by the country's ruling generals—including Than Shwe and the powerful intelligence chief Khin Nyunt—on numerous occasions in an effort to make him work with the junta and silence his opposition. But despite attempts by the military regime to win his respect, he always managed to keep his distance from the country's powerful leaders and refused to show them any sort of admiration.

Suu Kyi's trip to see Thamanya Sayadaw after her release from house arrest in 1995, therefore, was not just a religious pilgrimage. She wanted to show both the generals and her supporters that the sangha was supporting her rather than them, and when a photo of Suu Kyi sitting with the revered monk spread throughout the Burmese community both inside and outside the country, it was clear she had accomplished her task.

The good relationship that Suu Kyi had cultivated with the sangha was evident during the monk-led Saffron Revolution in 2007, when a group of monks peacefully walked toward Suu Kyi's house on September 22. They were initially stopped by the police, but then allowed to proceed, and when they arrived at her lakeside compound Suu Kyi briefly appeared at the gate with tears in her eyes to pay respect to them. The photo of Suu Kyi's brief meeting with the monks spread rapidly among the Burmese, touching the already raw nerves of the generals. Days later, the regime ordered troops to open fire on monks and demonstrators. After the Saffron Revolution, the sangha fell partially under the control of the military regime, which then attempted to flush out "pro-democracy monks." State media has repeatedly declared that monks should not be involved in politics and those who are should be considered "fake monks."[65]

Some of these "fake monks" include U Zawana, an activist monk who became politically involved at the time of the 1988 uprising and was first arrested during the 1990 *patta ni kozana kan*, said that after spending sixteen years in prison for his resistance work he was released to a completely different sangha. He said that the government-supported monk union, the State Sangha Maha Nayaka Committee, "has gained more control, and it is impossible for a monk like me to register again as a monk."[66] Another pro-democracy monk, Ashin Issariya, whose pen name is King Zero and who was a monk leader during the Saffron Revolution, said sinister tactics are employed to monitor the monasteries. Government-sponsored monks who are equivalent to spies have been placed in monasteries associated with pro-democracy activities, and the regime has given gifts such as cars, televisions, and mobile phones to senior monks in order to win their support.[67] Despite this blatant bribery, he remained diplomatic. "It is not the monks' fault; they don't have enough education and are exploited by the generals," he said.[68]

The effect of the government on the sangha is one of the least talked about but most important issues Suu Kyi and the pro-democracy opposition have faced since her release in 2010. It is imperative to dissuade influential monks from becoming instruments of the regime and to reincorporate and reinvigorate the sangha as active members of the opposition force. This may be easier said than done. The regime is well aware of the damage that the monks can do when allowed to gain political momentum, and have gone to great lengths to ensure that there is no repeat of the Saffron Revolution. During the 2010 election, this was shown in full effect when the sangha was only conspicuous in its silence. This is due, in part, to the 2010 election laws that could be interpreted as completely prohibiting monks or any other religious person or organization from political activity. Although vague, the laws left many smaller political parties concerned that any contact with religious leaders and institutions could put them at risk of being disbanded.

Along with the strict election laws and the regime's infiltration of the monasteries, the role of monks in the 2010 election was limited by the fact that many leading monks were not available to participate. Following the Saffron Revolution, many monk leaders fled to Thailand, where they either remain in refugee camps or have been resettled in third countries. The exile-based Assistance Association for Political Prisoners (Burma) reported that until the January 2012 amnesty, more than 250 monks continued to serve lengthy prison sentences.

THE INTERNATIONAL COMMUNITY

The release of Suu Kyi from house arrest was not just a seminal event for the Burmese people, the international community was also optimistic that this was an indication of real change in Burma. Within two weeks of her release, Suu Kyi had spoken to US President Barack Obama, French President Nicolas Sarkozy, UN Secretary-General Ban Ki-moon, several ASEAN leaders, and fellow Nobel Peace Prize winners Archbishop Desmond Tutu and the Dalai Lama. However, Suu Kyi has cautioned the international community not to become complacent with Burma, as the nation still has a long way to go until it can be fully trusted by the intenational community. Despite her wariness, it appears she will find it difficult to stem the flow of the many private companies and governments all eager to invest in this resource-rich nation.

For the previous two decades, much of the West supported Suu Kyi and the Burmese opposition through a combination of economic sanctions and diplomatic isolation of the regime, which she approved of and encouraged despite also being a consistent advocate of constructive dialogue. "She has always espoused engagement," NLD spokesman Nyan Win said on behalf of Suu Kyi while she was still under house arrest. "However, she suggested that engagement has to be done with both sides—the government as well as the democratic forces."[69] Towards the end of her house arrest, however, several factors conspired to dilute this strategy. One major example was that the Obama administration, along with much of the wider international community, renaged on its policy of isolating Burma and began to initiate a policy of fuller engagement with the junta in the dual beliefs that the strategy of isolating Burma had been unsuccessful and that dialogue could convince the generals to change their ways in order to negotiate the removal of sanctions.

Upon her release, Suu Kyi was faced with an international political and economic landscape that was very different from the time she was last free to speak with foreign leaders, and as a result she was forced to review her own cautious position on engagement and sanctions. As proof of this, one of the first things that Suu Kyi did after being released was say she would like to meet with Than Shwe. She also reasserted, however, that those countries wishing to engage would still need to remain watchful and not expect too much from the regime.

On the surface, the substance of the international engagement policy has been to encourage credible, democratic reforms: the immediate release of all political prisoners, serious dialogue with opposition and ethnic minority groups, and the end to human rights abuses. Engaging the regime in Burma has long been an option as long as the regime had the political will, and as long as engagement produced a tangible outcome. Suu Kyi's previous wariness came not from closed-mindedness, but rather from personal experience telling her that engagement in the past had not been successful, that it was the generals who most often chose not to engage, not the opposition, and that when the generals did engage it was to promote a hidden political agenda or to create the illusion of progress for international consumption.

In the wake of the election and Suu Kyi's release, Burmese dissidents at home and abroad felt that Europe had begun to concede too much to the regime and was being naive in its blind engagement with the generals. They argued that the European front was falling apart, pointing to events such as the March 2011 closed-door meeting in Rangoon, in which, after being informed that EU ambassadors were planning to meet with Suu Kyi privately, German diplomats insisted they should not meet the NLD leader separately, but only together with representatives of other opposition parties. The German ambassador, together with his Belgian and Spanish colleagues, argued that other democratic and ethnic forces might be offended if it became public that Suu Kyi was being afforded special treatment. In response, the UK ambassador pushed for a separate meeting with Suu Kyi, stating that she was still the undisputed leader of the democratic opposition: a fact that EU member states should not deny. Germany, however, believed that the goal of such a meeting should be to seek a wide range of views from several interlocutors without favoring anyone in particular.

At the same time that these countries were attempting to engage the junta, the previously impoverished military government had discovered buried treasure in the form of oil and gas reserves that could add billions in foreign currency to its finances. In addition, the regime began selling off other state resources, including timber and minerals, to neighbors such as China, further increasing its income at the long-term expense of the country and its environment. This recent discovery undeniably made the sanctions against Burma, most of which were put in place in the 1990s and widened several times in the 2000s, seem less appealing to those foreign countries who had espoused them over the past two decades. Some countries seemed to regret taking this principled stance that had left Burma wide open to exploitation by less scrupulous companies in neighboring countries such as China and India, while keeping Western companies, for the most part, shut out of the rush to claim a share of the country's resources. As a result, after Suu Kyi's release, the chorus calling for the easing or removal of sanctions became deafening, and it was only a matter of time until they were removed.

In early 2011, ASEAN issued a statement declaring that the events of November 2010—the freeing of Suu Kyi and the holding of an election less than a week earlier—were "sure signs that the country is heading toward a more democratic system,"[70] and its rotating chair, Indonesian Foreign Minister Marty Natalegawa, said that the international community should respond by removing or easing sanctions against the country's ruling regime. Some countries in the EU had the same inclination. The EU had adopted a policy with respect to sanctions on Burma known as the Common Position, which included an arms embargo, targeted financial sanctions, and an EU-wide travel ban for senior members of the military regime and their family members. While the Common Position was legally binding on member countries, a leaked US diplomatic cable revealed that Italy, Spain, and Germany had long been advocating reengagement with Burma and the lifting of sanctions. This clearly showed that despite the Common Position, divided opinions on Burma were rife within the EU. The different opinions of some member states caused tension and confusion within the organization, and sent mixed signals to Burmese democratic forces inside and outside the country who felt the EU had failed to employ its full economic and political potential to produce a positive outcome in military-ruled Burma.

Within Burma itself opinions were also split. In addition to ASEAN and some European nations, two political parties in Burma added their voices to calls for Western powers to lift sanctions. Punitive measures were "not beneficial," said the National Democratic Force (NDF), which split from the NLD to contest the vote in 2010 and won sixteen seats in the new parliament and regional legislatures. The Democratic Party (Myanmar)

Which won three seats, agreed.[71] But senior NLD leader Win Tin said, "Such calls are dishonest and those who made them are merely toeing the line of the military regime."[72] He added that sanctions hurt the junta and its cronies, and helped the opposition in its struggle for democracy.

The rush to lift international trade sanctions on Burma in the wake of Suu Kyi's by-election victory on April 2, 2012, surprised even the most resolute reformist. The EU took just weeks to pass a one-year suspension of sanctions, agreed on April 24, the very day that Suu Kyi was invited to enter parliament for the first time. Most shockingly, it took the West's biggest advocate of the crippling economic measures, the United States, just two days after the by-election victory, until April 4, to lift their sanctions. Observers were stunned by this: how could the United States—famously rebuked by liberal political scientists in 1998 for imposing economic sanctions against half the world's population—have been convinced that democracy had taken an irreversible hold in Burma? "Myanmar has turned away from five decades of authoritarianism and has embarked on a bold process of political, social, and economic reform," the International Crisis Group said in a report titled "Reform in Myanmar: One Year On," which was released in April 2012. "Those in the West who have long called for such changes must now do all they can to support them. The most important step is to lift the sanctions on Myanmar without delay."

Admittedly, US President Barack Obama's administration did renew the JADE (Junta's Anti-Democratic Efforts) Act of 2008 for three more years in August 2012. But it also controversially allowed US firms to invest in the Myanmar Oil and Gas Enterprise (MOGE) despite huge concerns over its accountability and transparency. The motives for this were self-evident. Investing in MOGE was the only way to gain access to Burma's

US President Barack Obama talks to journalists after a meeting with Aung San Suu Kyi at her home in Rangoon (November 2012).

lucrative energy resources, and US companies feared losing out to foreign competitors if the restrictions were not lifted. The US was quick to point out that safeguards were going to be put in place, with firms having to register their dealings within sixty days.

This presented a marked departure from Suu Kyi—for decades the principle barometer for US policy on Burma—who had only just warned against allowing unfettered investment in the country's natural resources. Speaking at the International Labour Organisation (ILO) annual conference in Geneva in June 2012, Suu Kyi reminded them of this. "The Myanmar Oil and Gas Enterprise . . . with which all foreign participation in the energy sector takes place through joint venture arrangements, lacks both transparency and accountability at present,"[73] she said.

The international community has not just responded to Burma's political opening through the lifting of sanctions and increased investment, since the country has begun to appear more democratic and release more political prisoners, Thein Sein has even begun to receive international visitors. US Secretary of State Hilary Clinton made a landmark visit to Burma in December 2011, during which she held a meeting with Thein Sein in Naypyidaw and also visited Suu Kyi in Rangoon. Clinton's visit marked a new era in US-Burma relations. President Obama, who first announced Clinton's plans to visit Burma, hailed policies by Thein Sein as leading the country "on the path toward reform,"[74] citing the government's cooperation with Suu Kyi, the release of political prisoners, and the relaxation of media restrictions as evidence. "These are the most important steps toward reform in Burma that we've seen in years," said Obama. Despite this praise, the US president also mentioned that these reforms marked only "flickers of progress" in the country.[75] The United States, he said, remained concerned about ongoing human rights abuses, the persecution of democratic reformers, and brutality toward ethnic minorities. In Rangoon, Clinton held a high-profile press conference with Suu Kyi as well as a series of meetings with opposition parties, ethnic groups, and civil society organizations. Suu Kyi called for the US to promote responsible investment in Burma, and the US finally eased sanctions and allowed American investors to enter the country. Finally, the US Senate confirmed the appointment of diplomat Derek Mitchell as the United States' first ambassador to the country for twenty-two years.

In November 2012, President Obama himself visited Burma during his tour of Southeast Asia, as part of which he also attended the ASEAN Summit in Cambodia. The US president, who had recently been re-elected for a second term, spent six hours in Rangoon, although he did not visit Naypyidaw. The visit demonstrated that Burma is no longer a pariah state. However, it still has a long way to go to be fully trusted by the international community. To US policy makers, Burma's move from authoritarian rule to "democracy" has been welcomed, and the visit was also seen as a political achievement for Obama after his re-election in November 2012.

Suu Kyi however, was intially said to have opposed Obama's visit to Burma.[76] She, as well as other activists and political observers, believed that Obama's trip was premature, although others argued that it was designed to embolden the people of Burma. To some political analysts the trip could also have been seen as part of a subtle US policy aiming to pull Burma away from the influence of China.

From a purely profit-driven perspective, it is hard to blame Western countries and companies for wanting to become involved in Burma. China, Thailand, India, Singapore, and South Korea are already heavily invested in Burma's primary industries, and new opportunities are opening up in other sectors such as manufacturing. Chinese companies alone invested US$8 billion in Burma in the first six months of 2010, mostly in gas, oil, and hydroelectric development projects. And neighboring Thailand has even bigger ambitions, with plans to develop a US$13.4 billion deep-sea port and industrial zone in Dawei (Tavoy), a town in southern Burma, that is expected to transform the area into a major transport and manufacturing hub.[77]

In her first major international speech following her release, Suu Kyi spoke for the first time about investment opportunities in Burma. In an articulate prerecorded message for the World Economic Forum held in January 2011, Suu Kyi lauded the potential for investment in Burma to a gathering of world leaders, businessmen, politicians, academics, and civil society representatives. Suu Kyi also requested that those who have invested or who are thinking of investing in Burma should put a premium on respect for the law, on environmental and social factors, on the rights of workers, on job creation, and on the promotion of technological skills. She said that she would like to speak on behalf of the 55 million people of Burma whom she acknowledged have been left behind while their country's neighbors developed economic ties with the junta and exploited the country's abundant natural resources. "We yearn to be a part of the global community: not only to be economically and socially connected, but also to achieve the domestic political stability and national reconciliation that would enable us to fully address the needs of our people," she said.[78]

Suu Kyi has the key to open many doors. Her message to the international audience has long been that her country needs to be part of the global community and she is in no doubt that it is time to cautiously shed Burma's pariah status. What is missing from the discussion, however, is any proof that investment will improve lives in a country that was once one of the most developed in the region but was then reduced to a shambles by its inept and avaricious rulers. While cautious engagement with the new government may be appropriate, there is currently no reason to believe that the lifting of the sanctions that occurred in April 2012 will serve any purpose other than to enrich Western corporations and, of course, the generals and their cronies.

THE UNITED NATIONS

After the brutal military crackdown in 1988, UN special envoys began jetting in and out of Burma engaging Burma's stakeholders, the regime, and the opposition, and each time, they left the country empty-handed. It is not, therefore, surprising to learn that the long-oppressed Burmese people have had little cause to have faith in the UN and its effort to bring reconciliation and dialogue between Suu Kyi and the regime. Even worse, UN envoys have sometimes become part of the problem, utilizing the regime's propaganda phrases while Burma sank deeper into political, economic, and social crisis. A big question in many minds within Burma, therefore, has long been how the UN has been able to play such a key role in the democracy movement and the ethnic conflict while acheiving so little over so long.

Following Suu Kyi's release in 2010, UN Secretary-General Ban Ki-moon issued a statement saying, "Her dignity and courage in the face of injustice have been an inspiration to many people around the world, including the secretary-general, who has long advocated her freedom."[79] Against a background of UN inaction, many Burmese saw this as a poor choice of words after decades of missed opportunities within Burma—the final clause even appeared to hint that the UN's current top diplomat was taking partial credit for Suu Kyi's release. The statement also retroactively criticized the regime: "Notwithstanding the welcome news of her release, it is deeply regrettable that Daw Aung San Suu Kyi was effectively excluded from participating in the recent elections."[80] This statement was probably not enough to placate Burma's opposition, which had been lobbying the

UN for years to take a more aggressive stance with respect to the junta. As a result, despite its proclaimed advocacy on behalf of democracy and human rights in Burma, the UN long ago lost its standing among the Burmese pro-democracy and human rights movement, who believe that the UN's top-down approach of trying to pressure the regime leaders by issuing statements, releasing progress reports, and dispatching envoys has borne no results in the past and will not do so in the future.

Most believe that UN chief Ban Ki-moon has been less than forceful about advocating democracy in Burma. Although, as the junta geared up for the 2010 election, he did convene several "Group of Friends" meetings to discuss the situation. In his meetings with ASEAN leaders, the UN chief also made passionate appeals to help move Burma toward democracy.[81] In the end, Ban Ki-moon was unsuccessful in pushing the military regime to allow Suu Kyi and other pro-democracy leaders to participate in the election and, as throughout the past years of failed efforts, the Burmese people once again saw the UN as hopelessly ineffective in bringing real change to the country. The diplomatic jargon, endless expressions of "concern," and repetition of such clichés as "progress," "tangible results," "turning a new page," and "cautious optimism," no longer had any meaning to the Burmese; they have even become the target of ridicule by Burmese cartoonists.

In April 2000, Razali Ismail was appointed UN special envoy to Burma. He was from the region so he could understand the country's situation well and the generals could trust him. In fact, the Malaysian diplomat's effort to bring about a political settlement in Burma was initially met with positive feedback. But he came under fire for facilitating ongoing secret talks in Rangoon between the ruling military leaders and Suu Kyi. And later, when no progress was seen in his mission, Burmese observers became increasingly impatient with what appeared to be stalled negotiations, causing many to question exactly what Razali was accomplishing in Rangoon.

In 2002, the *International Herald Tribune* reported that a business contract between the Burmese government and Iris Technologies, in which Razali was reported to own a 30 percent stake, was signed during the time he was conducting his diplomatic mission.[82] Upon learning the news the UN declared that there was no conflict of interest, but the damage had been done; Razali's credibility as negotiator and facilitator had been compromised. In January 2006, Razali Ismail quit his post after having being refused entry into Burma for nearly two years. He said it was clear the military generals "do not want me back."[83]

In the eyes of most Burmese, Ibrahim Gambari, a Nigerian diplomat who succeeded Razali and was the UN special envoy to Burma from 2006 until 2009, was an especially egregious failure. The Burmese ridiculed the UN missions that went nowhere under his guidance, costing the UN credibility and lessening its effectiveness. Gambari was ill-informed and naively upbeat on Burma's often bleak political progress, and his inappropriate claims of success regarding political negotiations with the junta only drew anger. During many of his visits to Burma, Gambari was shunned by Than Shwe and was virtually a prisoner of the government, staying in isolated Naypyidaw and following a regime-ordained itinerary that included attendance at a rally in Shan State denouncing the September 2007 pro-democracy uprising. All of his facetime with junta officials was spent receiving history lectures on how the regime had created the country, and Gambari's missions accomplished almost nothing.[84] Tellingly, during Gambari's 2008 visit to Burma, Suu Kyi turned down a request for a meeting; her party colleagues later said she was unhappy with the way his mission was being organized and carried out.[85] Critics of his performance note that the number of political prisoners in Burma nearly doubled in the years after his appointment as the special envoy in 2006, a fact that drew little response from Gambari. As a result, he was unpopular with the many Burmese languishing in prisons who believed he was doing a disservice to their country. Gambari was reassigned in 2009.

Then, in late 2010, UN Secretary-General Ban Ki-moon's chief of staff, Vijay Nambiar, was named as replacement.[86] While Nambiar was more respected by the Burmese opposition than his predecessor, Burma had long been a political graveyard for UN and other international negotiators. With this certainly in mind, Nambiar flew into Burma shortly after the release of Suu Kyi to meet her. Suu Kyi described her meeting with

Nambiar as "very valuable," but added that they might need "many and frequent meetings to sort out all the problems we are facing."[87] He also met some junta officials, including Foreign Minister Nyan Win. He was unable, however, to meet with Than Shwe or any other senior regime leaders. On his return, Nambiar said he was encouraged by the openness exhibited by military authorities in Burma, adding that he was allowed to meet with anybody he wanted to in the country. He also said that the junta needed to consider political transformation that includes elements previously excluded from the government.[88] He said, "There is a role for the United Nations, both in the context of the political developments as well as the broader context of the socio-economic development."[89] While acknowledging that the Burmese government saw the increasing role of the UN as a way of convincing the international community to remove the sanctions and aid Burma's economic development, he said he believed that the government received his message.

The efforts of the UN advisers were not enough to placate the international community. A frustrated Aung Din, director of the US Campaign for Burma in Washington DC, said on the "Groups of Friends" meeting held by Ban Ki-moon, "As long as Ban Ki-moon does not assert his moral authority and demand these nations exercise a collective and effective pressure on the regime, this meeting will be nothing more than another public relations show by the UN."[90] He added that the military regime in Burma did not care about hollow threats, it would be affected only by actions such as a UN Commission of Inquiry and a total rejection of the sham election.

Many, like Aung Din, realized that without forceful consequences it would be better not to simply talk to the generals in the hope that they could be coaxed into change. With that as well as justice in mind, the US Campaign for Burma, along with several other organizations, pressed the world body for a Commission of Inquiry into war crimes and crimes against humanity against the military junta. This subsequently gained support from a host of Western countries including the United States, Britain, Canada, and France. In March 2010, Tomas Ojea Quintana, an Argentine lawyer who became the special human rights investigator for the UN in Burma in May 2008, issued a report also recommending that the UN convene the Commission of Inquiry.[91] This earned him a brief visa ban from the regime. But Quintana was undaunted by the snub, and less than two weeks before the election he presented his annual report to the UN General Assembly that highlighted the plight of specific political prisoners and cases of human rights abuses.

On July 31, 2012, Quintana made a trip to Burma's western Arakan State to assess the humanitarian situation following sectarian violence between Arakan Buddhists and Rohingya Muslims. His trip was well received by the international community and publicized by the Burmese government in its attempts to counter allegations of human rights abuses. Yet, Buddhists across Burma took to the streets to protest his visit in the belief that the Argentine would back the Muslim Rohingya's allegations of state-sponsored brutality. Evidently, mistrust of the UN remains pervasive in Burmese society.

Despite Quintana's individual qualities and efforts, due to past experience there are still few members of the Burmese opposition movement who take the UN seriously. It is always expected that whenever Ban Ki-moon convenes a Burma meeting in New York attended by top diplomats, the UN will issue a statement expressing its concern over the current situation. Yet, up until the present, the regime has been immune from any effective UN action and therefore has virtually ignored the international body.

The threat of a Commission of Inquiry seems to have been put on the backburner since Suu Kyi's reentry into Burmese politics and her insistance on restitutive rather than retaliatory justice. Yet, the generals are well aware of what happened to dictators in the Middle East following the 2011 Arab Spring, as well as to Milosevic and others brought to justice for war crimes following the break up of the former Yugoslavia. The proposed Commission of Inquiry, therefore, may have been sidelined or sacrificed to avoid derailing the current process of reform.

3

THE UNFINISHED STRUGGLE

THE THEIN SEIN GOVERNMENT: A TURNING POINT?

Despite the fraudulent election that propelled President Thein Sein to power, his new government, to the surprise of many, has since introduced many initiatives and heralded a political opening for a raft of long-term dissenters. But does anyone believe that this former general and the government he commands are sincere and committed to popular rule? Further, if they are committed to reform, how can they implement their policies with the ever-present shadow of Than Shwe and his loyal military on the sidelines?

Thein Sein is regarded by many as a moderate, although his history suggests he is no benign, civilian leader. He was a close confidant of Than Shwe from the very beginning of the dictator's rule, and his absolute loyalty could never be questioned. Thein Sein served as part of the secretive inner circle of one of the world's most brutal regimes, and under the shadow of Than Shwe he was merely a puppet. No one knew of Thein Sein's political ambition and his vision for the country. He kept his thoughts to himself. Even Burma-watchers who had some limited access to the inner circle of the regime had little to say about him. A 2007 US embassy cable described

President Thein Sein (Naypyidaw, May 2012)

him as a "consummate insider." What is clear is that without Than Shwe's blessing and trust, he would not have been given the highest position in government.

Those who know the current president claim he is a mild-mannered and quiet individual. Retired Lieutenant-General Chit Swe, under whom Thein Sein served in the 1980s, described him as someone who rarely shows his emotions, is notably devoid of arrogance, and is usually willing to listen to differing opinions.[1] He is also noted for his relative compassion for the suffering of the Burmese people. When Cyclone Nargis slammed into the Irrawaddy Delta in 2008 and Than Shwe's government blocked significant amounts of foreign aid to the area, Thein Sein was the first top general to travel there and meet victims. He is also said to have "appealed directly" to Than Shwe to belatedly allow foreign aid workers into the disaster zone.[2] Thein Sein manages to demonstrate a degree of sensitivity that nearly all his fellow generals lack. It is a trait that seems at odds with his position at the helm of essentially the same ruthless regime that gunned down unarmed monks and demonstrators during the 2007 Saffron Revolution.

Over the past two years, under Thein Sein and his new government, Burma has seen a political opening that has caught critics and skeptics by surprise. The new Burmese government has taken more steps toward political reform than the previous military regime managed in over two decades. This reform has not been to everyone within the party's liking, however, and has been achieved while Thein Sein's administration has faced significant opposition from within. In May 2012, he openly warned government hardliners during a meeting in Naypyidaw that "conservatives who do not have a reformist mindset will be left behind."[3] Several senior government officials also admitted that the president received only minority backing from the cabinet and faced hurdles in implementing his reform program. Perhaps it was tackling internal divisions while guiding the fragile democratic transition that forced Thein Sein and his reform-minded colleagues to seek out new allies.

Since he became president, Thein Sein has called for cooperation and urged the country's authorities to respect the rights of citizens. In January 2012, the government freed several prominent political prisoners including Min Ko Naing and Ko Ko Gyi, as well as many other former student activists, although there are still many who remain behind bars. He has also reached out to ethnic insurgents, initiated discussions about legalizing trade unions, and loosened the government's tight grip on censorship. The self-proclaimed reformist has repeatedly stressed the need for good and clean governance, and has promised to fight the endemic corruption that so blights the nation.

Thein Sein has matched his words with his actions, to some extent, although state-sponsored brutality and undemocratic actions hinder progress. He suspended the controversial China-funded dam project in Kachin State, and the decision receieved kudos from the Beijing-wary United States in particular. In his press release, he explained that the decision was based on a desire to protect the environment and listen to public opinion.

However, in late November 2012, the government's pre-dawn raid on copper mine protesters dealt a major blow to Thein Sein's credibility. Dozens of monks were seriously injured and senior ministers attached to the President's Office had to personally apologize to monks and an angry public.

There are further questions as to what extent Thein Sein is truly in control of Burma and whether his hold on power is safe from power-hungry former military generals. In a March 2012 speech, Thein Sein addressed parliament on the first anniversary of his government assuming power. The speech, which was broadcast live on the state-run MRTV television station, was generally well received by most Burmese. However, some longtime political observers were more skeptical, noting that the president appeared to be papering over a number of issues that could undermine his efforts to deliver further reforms. He also surprised many by mentioning the political aspirations of Burma's ethnic minorities, an issue that has resulted in more than six decades of unresolved conflict, saying, "As our country is a union nation, we must let all ethnic minorities get equally involved in the political process . . . It is necessary that we, the current government, help to end the misunderstanding and mistrust between ethnic groups and the government."[4]

In one of the more unexpected turns in his speech, Thein Sein also mentioned the desire of many young ethnic soldiers to possess weapons better suited to the information age. "According to a young, ethnic, armed leader, young, ethnic, armed people aged eighteen and nineteen often say they also want to hold laptops, computers. I was very sad to hear this. I have decided to eliminate all these misfortunes during my administration,"[5] he said.

Any one of these developments—and especially the last—could easily be seized upon by hardliners as a pretext for reversing democratization in the name of national security. Sidelining Thein Sein and his relatively small group of fellow reformers would not be difficult, particularly considering that he is already sixty-seven.

This precarious democracy is matched with further questions about the continuing role of Than Shwe. Thein Sein and ministers continue to meet the former leader at his large compound in Naypyidaw, and, according to several political sources, Than Shwe has maintained his regular contact with the top brass in the armed forces and hardline allies in the government and the parliament. The current military commander-in-chief Senior General Min Aung Hlaing is said to be loyal to Than Shwe, and he continues to exercise his control over major reshuffles in the armed forces. Thein Sein, who is now a civilian president, seems to have little control over the military. When the military increased its offensive in northern Burma to include the deployment of jet fighters against Kachin insurgents near the Chinese border, Thein Sein's calls to halt the offensive were ignored.

In an interview with *The Associated Press* in 2012, Suu Kyi affirmed that the generals still wield enormous power despite the veneer of democracy provided by the elections: "I am concerned about how much support there is in the military for changes," she said. "In the end that's the most important factor—how far the military are prepared to cooperate with reform principles."[6] This may be why Suu Kyi has repeatedly emphasized that Burma is still far from the point of no return, saying in February 2012, "Many people are beginning to say that the democratization process here is irreversible. It's not so."[7]

If, indeed, the new president and his reform-minded allies really intend to put Burma permanently on the path to democracy, decisive action must be taken against those within his own ranks who are opposed to his long-term goals. Words and goodwill will only take him so far. Nonetheless, Thein Sein appears to be the most morally responsible head of state that Burma has experienced in more than half a century, and his reforms have led many to believe that Burma may, one day, experience the genuine democracy that the opposition movement has long been fighting for.

SUU KYI TAKES CENTER STAGE

General Aung San was a determined and pragmatic leader who drew ideas and inspiration from many sources and was willing to use every means at his disposal to achieve Burmese independence from the British. He posthumously achieved that goal for his beloved people, only for dictators such as Ne Win and Than Shwe to snatch it away. His daughter Suu Kyi and all of those involved in the pro-democracy movement have been fighting Than Shwe and the current regime for two decades in what Suu Kyi has called Burma's "second struggle for independence."[8]

It is clear that Suu Kyi has taken the baton in Aung San's unfinished race. But, as she admitted, those engaged in the second struggle have faced an entirely different set of challenges than those her father faced in opposing the brutal, homegrown dictators who serve in the army she proudly claims her father founded. To achieve real democracy and equality, Suu Kyi has the unenviable task of persuading the many factions involved in Burma's struggle to unite and work together for one common goal. Even more difficult will be the necessity for all of these factions to unite behind Suu Kyi herself, putting their grievances, both about political issues and about her personally, to one side for the benefit of all Burma. This may not be as simple as Suu Kyi may hope and currently there are grave doubts about whether the democracy leader can realistically represent the diverse interests of the 55 million people of Burma. The struggle is by no means over, and Suu Kyi, her colleagues, and her critics, still face a long road to democracy.

Since she accepted the terms of the constitution and entered parliament in April 2012, Suu Kyi's actions, speeches, and meetings have been under close scrutiny for the extent to which she has has been successful in bringing together the various factions of the NLD and the rest of the democracy movement into one cohesive group, and the extent to which she is representing the best interests of the Burmese people.

May and June 2012 were busy months for Suu Kyi as she made her first overseas trip in twenty-four years. While a largely successful visit, the events did not pass without scrutiny and criticism, both from political opponents and Burmese allies. At the end of May she traveled to Thailand to attend the World Economic Forum, and asked global leaders to exercise "healthy skepticism,"[9] as her country began to take steps to shed half a century of military rule. President Thein Sein was also invited to attend the forum but canceled at the last moment. Although he officially attributed his absense to "solving domestic crises at home,"[10] press reports suggested that the president did not want to be upstaged by Suu Kyi.

Residents of Mae La refugee camp celebrate Aung San Suu Kyi's historic visit (June 2012).

Following her meeting in Bangkok, Suu Kyi went to meet Burmese migrant workers in Mahachai, 45 kilometers southwest of Bangkok, and then flew to Mae Sot where she visited some of the thousands of her compatriots living as refugees on Thai soil—a visit that drew some criticism.

With a population of forty thousand mainly ethnic Karen, Mae La is the largest of the nine refugee camps dotted along the mountainous Thai-Burmese border. The inhabitants began preparing for Suu Kyi's arrival before dawn, decorating the camp and hanging pictures of Suu Kyi and her illustrious father in front of their bamboo and wooden houses. Mae La is no stranger to Nobel laureates: seven Peace Prize winners including Archbishop Desmond Tutu and former Costa Rican resident Oscar Arias visited in 1993 to express solidarity for Suu Kyi while she was under house arrest. Nevertheless, this was a historic visit. Suu Kyi has always repeated her commitment to fundamental change in Burma, including a federal union, and so the ethnic Karen refugees received her with open arms.

However, a large number of people were left disappointed by their access to the democracy leader. When Suu Kyi's convoy finally arrived, a heavily armed security detail arranged by the Thai police blocked well-wishers from getting close.

In June, Suu Kyi flew further afield, to Europe. First she stopped in Oslo to receive the Nobel Peace Prize, twenty-one years after having the award bestowed. Opening the ceremony in Oslo, the chairman of the Norwegian Nobel Committee, Thorbjorn Jagland, said, "Dear Aung San Suu Kyi, we have been waiting for you for a very long time. However, we are well aware that your wait has been infinitely trying for you and one entirely of a different nature from ours."

Wearing a traditional Burmese gown of lilac and ivory, Suu Kyi told the audience,

> When the Nobel Committee awarded the Peace Prize to me they were recognizing that the oppressed and the isolated in Burma were also a part of the world, they were recognizing the oneness of humanity. So for me receiving the Nobel Peace Prize means personally extending my concerns for democracy and human rights beyond national borders. The Nobel Peace Prize opened up a door in my heart.
>
> The potential of our country is enormous. This should be nurtured and developed to create not just a more prosperous but also a more harmonious, democratic society where our people can live in peace, security, and freedom.

During her European tour, she also stopped in Switzerland, Ireland, England, and France. In Dublin, Suu Kyi shared the stage with Bono, the controversial U2 frontman, who dedicated the song "Walk On" to her struggle for democracy.

In London, as she was greeted by British Prime Minister David Cameron at his official 10 Downing Street residence, Suu Kyi recalled her father being photographed outside the famous house, wrapped in a large British military-issue coat to protect against the cold. She told MPs,

I have just come from Downing Street. It was my first visit there.
And yet, for me, it was a familiar scene, not just from television
broadcasts, but from my own family history. As some of you may
be aware, the best known photograph of my father Aung San,
taken shortly before his assassination in 1947, was of him standing
in Downing Street with Clement Atlee and others with whom he had
been discussing Burma's transition to independence. He was pictured
wearing a large British military-issue greatcoat. This had been given
to him by Jawaharlal Nehru en route to the UK, to protect against
the unaccustomed cold. And I must say, having not left my tropical
country for twenty-four years, there have been the odd moments
this week when I have thought of that coat myself.[11]

She was later photographed occupying the same spot in which her
father had stood more than half-a-century earlier.

At a news conference with Suu Kyi, Cameron pledged his support for
the ongoing reform process in Burma. "In order for that to succeed we
have to work with the regime," he said, and Suu Kyi instructed the British
prime minister, "More than ever we need our friends to be watchdogs.
You have to watch what is going on in Burma."[12]

Suu Kyi then made a historic address in London to a joint session of
both Houses of Parliament, where she commented on Burma's recent
by-elections:

Our by-elections were held on April 1 and I am conscious that there
was a certain skepticism that this would be another elaborate April
Fools joke. In fact, it turned out to be an April of new hope. The
voting process was largely free and fair and I would like to pay
tribute to President Thein Sein for this, and for his committment
and sincerity in the reform process.[13]

She also briefly touched on the issue of sectarian violence between
Arakanese Buddhists and Rohingya Muslims in Arakan State that had
broken out a few days earlier. "In over sixty years of independence,

Burma has not yet known a time when we could say that there was peace throughout the land," said Suu Kyi. "At this very moment, hostilities continue between Kachin forces and the state armed forces in the north. In the west, communal strife has led to the loss of innocent lives and the displacements of tens of thousands of hapless citizens. We need to address the problems that lie at the root of the conflict."[14]

Despite mentioning the crisis, the ethnic issues that so plague Burma are one of the biggest challenges Suu Kyi faces, and she has come under increasing criticism for the position that she has taken regarding the Rohingya issue.

In October 2012, fresh violence broke out between Arakanese and the Rohingya. Dozens of people were killed and several thousands fled native towns and villages. The violence seriously undermined the recent political opening in Burma. Suu Kyi was again in the spotlight. People wanted to hear her reaction and how she would stop the bloodshed and violence. She told the BBC in November, "I am urging tolerance but I do not think one should use one's moral leadership, if you want to call it that, to promote a particular cause without really looking at the sources of the problems . . . I know that people want me to take one side or the other, so both sides are displeased because I will not take a stand with them."[15] Many believe that Suu Kyi could play a crucial role in easing the hatred and raise much-needed awareness of the plight of the Rohingya. But the Nobel laureate has remained largely mute on the issue, as in this instance, and has even endorsed her NLD party position that the Rohingya do not deserve Burmese citizenship—a seemingly irreconcilable viewpoint considering the decades she has spent championing human rights.

Her failure to exercise her moral leadership to intervene in the sectarian violence has caused observers and activists alike to speculate on her motives. One, Maung Zarni, a Burma activist and visiting fellow at the London School of Economics, ventured that "Politically, Aung San Suu Kyi has absolutely nothing to gain from opening her mouth on this . . . She is no longer a political dissident trying to stick to her principles. She's a politician and her eyes are fixed on the prize, which is the 2015 majority Buddhist vote."[16] Perhaps Suu Kyi has resolved to play the political game and not fall into the trap of championing essentially unpopular policies, even at the expense of her own convictions.

Indeed, former student activists, politicians, and exiled activists have maintained respect and political support for Suu Kyi, but many have quietly expressed that Suu Kyi has increasingly become a more self-interested politician, who, due to her failure to criticize the ongoing offensive in Kachin State, is swiftly losing support from ethnic minorities. Several exiled activists and scholars who returned to Burma were refused meetings with her. To the astonishment of many, some of them even decided to work for the government and President Thein Sein. However, on the even more contentious issue of the Rohingya, most activists and scholars seemed to think she was wise not to say too much.

Critics also argue that Suu Kyi's connection to the military has affected the way that she relates to the regime. She has said that she does not want to see the military disintegrate completely, but rather she wants to see an army and an organization that is "rising to dignified heights of professionalism and patriotism"[17]—a wish that many believe is also widely held among military personnel themselves and their family members. Some in the opposition movement see Suu Kyi's military family history as a two-sided coin—as both an asset and a liability. While Suu Kyi has obviously suffered greatly at the hands of Than Shwe and his regime, her family association with the *Tatmadaw* has also benefited her in certain respects, a fact which causes conflict and resentment for other, more harshly treated, dissidents.

It is a two-way relationship. Because she is the daughter of Burma's independence hero, the generals have claimed in the past that they see her like a younger sister—which many dissidents believe is an intentionally patronizing statement—and most likely this was why she was allowed to serve her incarceration at her lakeside home rather than in a remote prison like many other political detainees. As evidence of this, in 2009, a letter from Than Shwe read aloud in the Insein courtroom where Suu Kyi was being tried for harboring John Yettaw, the American who swam to her home, stated that because she was the daughter of national hero

Aung San her sentence would be reduced from three years of hard labor to eighteen months under house arrest.

In 2010, the regime snubbed many prominent political prisoners—including some introduced in previous chapters, Min Ko Naing and Ko Ko Gyi, as well as Htay Kywe, Pyone Cho, and Min Zeya—when it decided to free Suu Kyi but keep them behind bars, possibly because they were feared more than Suu Kyi. Former political prisoners have, therefore, accused Suu Kyi of being a celebrity who does not understand prison life and cannot truly comprehend the deep suffering of the Burmese people and the brutal nature of the regime. They say that unlike Aung San, she is seen now as indecisive, cautious, and as not truly understanding either the political landscape of the country or the brutal military mentality.

Ironically, Suu Kyi's newfound reticence could also be seen as a good thing. For decades, she was often faulted for putting principles before pragmatism; for example during the 2010 election when with she argued that the NLD should not take part. But at the same time, she was also trailed by critics who noted that her stance on the burning ethnic issues at that time left a great deal to be desired.

In September 2012, Suu Kyi made a seventeen-day visit to the US to receive a top honor award, the Congressional Gold Medal, in Washington DC. Suu Kyi described the ceremony as being one of the most moving days of her life. During her tour, she also met President Obama, then Secretary of State Hilary Clinton, and several political heavyweights including Senator John McCain, Senator Mitch McConnell, and Madeleine Albright. Many noted that during her trip to the United States, which coincided with a separate visit by President Thein Sein, Suu Kyi was careful to avoid sending any messages that would conflict with his. Once the perennial dissident, Suu Kyi appears to be now actively working with the government.

During his US trip, Thein Sein spoke on the BBC Hardtalk program. When asked whether the constitution could be altered to accept Suu Kyi as president in Burma if the people elected her, Thein Sein answered, "Amending the constitution cannot be done by myself alone . . . the constitution has provisions of how to amend the constitution and parliament and people need to support it." When pressed further, the president evaded the question. Not surprisingly, Thein Sein was also very vague when the BBC pressed him several times about whether he had any regret for the past repressive policies of the regime. Thein Sein said in response, "Our reforms have been welcomed, that's why they have been put in place," and when pressed further only said, "They were acting on their beliefs and we were acting on our beliefs. . . . Everyone was working for the country in their own way."

Suu Kyi is understandably more anxious for constitutional reform than the current president. Upon returning from her US trip, she said at a press conference, "As the leader of a political party, I have the courage to be president, if the people so wish." She then added that the constitution must be amended because "it's part of the parliamentary process. We will keep pushing for it. Not just for me, but for the country."[18]

The constitution is not the only obstacle in front of Suu Kyi in her bid to become the leader of the nation. Another more daunting hurdle must also be cleared: Suu Kyi must unite the disparate factions of the NLD and provide them with genuine leadership.

The NLD, the party Suu Kyi helped found in 1988, has come under fire for its reputation of comprising primarily Suu Kyi loyalists, and for its failure to reach out to other influential groups in Burmese society, including returning exiles and intellectuals. Despite its resounding victory in by-elections, the NLD's management and public relations have been criticized, and there appear to be few mechanisms with which to attract and cultivate real political talent. Suu Kyi, who will be seventy years old by the time Burma is ready to go to the polls again in 2015, has given no hint of who her political successor will be and no one in her party stands out as a likely candidate.

There is little doubt that Suu Kyi still enjoys enormous support among Burma's people, despite questions among some about her commitment to the country's minorities, her indecisiveness, and a lack of reform within the NLD. Many in the opposition movement remain hopeful, although they know that the country lacks strong democratic institutions and instead depends on figureheads such as Suu Kyi, the 88 Generation Students, and the ethnic leaders.

The changes that Burma has experienced within the past few years may not be permanent, and shifts in leadership can still lead to chaotic political upheaval, giving the army cause to step in and return to repressive rule. Less dramatically, the government and military can stall the transition process for as long as they see fit while still benefiting from dropped sanctions and increased engagement. It is still too early to say whether Burma will have a functioning democracy or a weak pseudo-democracy.

HOMECOMING

After being in exile for twenty-four years, my dream of being able to return home was finally fulfilled when I was given a five-day journalist visa to enter Burma at the end of January 2012, despite being told that I would remain on the blacklist.

I was excited but also determined to remain calm and not invite disappointment. I had lived more than half my life in exile and had started to wonder if I would even recognize my own country. I had, however, always felt distinctly Burmese and had regular dreams of returning home during my two decades in exile. As a journalist, I had watched and reported on Burmese events since the early 1990s and had never felt that I had missed any major breaking news in the country. But now I could set my feet on the ground and was convinced that it would provide me with an alternative perspective and make my reporting more dynamic.

As the plane descended towards Rangoon International Airport I noticed a slight change in my heartbeat. I felt calm, but also aware that I was about to return to where many friends and colleagues had suffered so terribly.

Although frequently attending conferences all around the world, I had always refused to live in the West despite having the opportunity to do so. By living in Thailand, I felt that I could contribute more to change in Burma through media work. My activities were, of course, different to my brief stint as a student activist in 1988, but I felt that by being in Thailand I was able to remain much closer to the grass-roots struggle. Even so, I still sometimes felt like I was far from my country.

Red tilled soil, green rice fields, pagodas, and bamboo huts occupied my view as we approached the runway. My plane was filled with tourists as well as several young Burmese working in the Middle East, Malaysia, and Europe who were returning to visit their families. Some spoke to me, saying that they read our website and knew the magazine. I smiled back and chatted as best I could. Was I nervous? I could not imagine how many years in prison the regime could give me because of my work. I began to count. The plane touched down. I was home.

Inside the airport, a young immigration officer smiled as I handed over my passport. He was quite talkative and he asked about *The Irrawaddy*: how we gather news from inside Burma, how we designed our website, and so on. With a smile that betrayed his betel-chewing habit—his teeth had a telltale tinge of red—he admitted visiting our website as often as possible. Meanwhile, the people in line behind me grew impatient as they were kept waiting until my cordial interrogation was finally over.

A TV crew from Al Jazeera came to film my arrival and were soon joined by Special Branch officers who also wielded cameras. They politely snapped a few photos as I smiled back. I jokingly told them to ensure their report to their superiors was completely accurate. They assured me that they would, asked me my age, and then left.

Upon leaving the airport I found I had arrived in a country that I did not know. Over the past two decades, the military dictators have raped this once beautiful and promising land. But on my way into the city from the airport I noticed one familiar face: Aung San. Aung San's image was plastered everywhere, as well as that of Suu Kyi and the insignia of her NLD. People felt able to speak freely and discussed politics in teashops as if the military had returned to their barracks and Burma already enjoyed full democracy. When meeting former generals and government officials I had mixed feelings. I met many who claimed to be reformists, but I felt in general that they were not genuine about reform. They appeared to be performing a role advocating reform rather than truly agreeing with it, and still believed that the military must remain in power. Many continued to live in the same manner as they had in the old system, and still enjoyed unelected power and enormous wealth. I also met several former generals who seemed to be excited to see changes taking place in the country, but they all worried about the future and the safety of their family members should their privileges be taken away. As a journalist, I was looking for substantive evidence that reform was taking place.

There were many other officials who were also worried that there would be a public backlash because the military had done so little for the country over the last half-century. I was shocked to see the abject poverty and suffering of ordinary people, and so many things fundamentally wrong with Burmese society, from the education system, to social and public health and endemic corruption. This further convinced me of the military regime's disastrous mismanagement of Burma, which has ruined not only the fabric of the country, but has also taken a toll on people's ethical values. Living under a military dictatorship for so many years has taught people to keep emotion and anger suppressed. While Rangoon's beautiful and historic buildings can be restored, how can we rebuild the nation's lost generations and repair the country's moral decline?

Indeed, the poverty I saw day-to-day made it even more surreal to visit some of the beautiful houses belonging to tycoons, replete with expensive racing cars and wine cellars worth millions of dollars.

My days in Rangoon during the 1980s were much cleaner and brighter, but since the government left the former capital and moved to newly-built Naypyidaw, the city has begun to fall into decline.

During my brief stay, I met Suu Kyi, Win Tin, Tin Oo, and Ko Ko Gyi, and traveled to Naypyidaw to speak with officials from the Ministry of Information. I also visited editors and journalists, and as many other people as possible. Of course, I made sure to go to Shwedagon Pagoda to pray for the recovery of my country and people, also wishing that the visit would not be my last.

My short meeting with Suu Kyi took place amid a large crowd in her chaotic party headquarters. People there were excited, and when I climbed the stairs Tin Oo and Win Tin were both cheerful. They smiled when I handed them *The Irrawaddy* magazine, and Win Tin sat and read silently while Tin Oo grinned and revealed how he received our publication from diplomatic sources when under house arrest. "I loved reading it, and when intelligence officers came to see me I would always hide it," he said. After a long wait, Suu Kyi saw me. She was extremely busy and obviously tense, but emphasized the need to keep up quality reporting even though we were based outside the country.

In meeting several senior journalists, I discovered that they harbored deep cynicism regarding the political opening within their country. Burmese society still suffers heavily from an absence of trust. No one has confidence in the military but Suu Kyi remains hugely popular. I found it was almost impossible to have a rational conversation about the NLD party's shortcomings or a critical analysis of the Nobel laureate.

My colleagues whom I had not seen for years were all well. Some were working with the NLD and civil society groups while others who have left politics were still keenly watching developments unfold. In general it seemed like they shared the same deep skepticism about the legitimacy of Burma's nascent democracy as those who work in the media.

On the last day of my trip, I followed Suu Kyi's first campaign tour to Kawhmu, the impoverished Irrawaddy Delta township where she was running for a seat in parliament. There is no doubt that for many Burmese, Suu Kyi remains their greatest hope for real, positive change. Everywhere, her supporters came out in force to wave as she made the grueling journey from Rangoon. Even a coffin that passed the crowds en route to the cemetery was bedecked with NLD flags. Suu Kyi's campaign platform was to amend the 2008 constitution, ensure the rule of law, and secure internal peace with ethnic armed groups. I could see the mood of those rallying behind her and fully understood their adoration of The Lady. But the question remained: can she alone bring change to the country?

I thought constantly about the opposition movement, the NLD, and Suu Kyi. Principally, I questioned whether Suu Kyi can transform herself from a dissident leader into a real political player in the union parliament after the NLD win the election in 2015? Is she ready to compromise? In politics, there are always trade-offs—indeed, the arts of negotiation and flexibility are even more vital in military-dominated Burma.

The author (*left*) reuniting with Maung Linn Yone, one of the leading figures of the Insein Sarpay Wine literature circle, after twenty-four years, in January 2012. Maung Linn Yone is a poet, writer, and teacher who was also a former student union activist in 1962 and was imprisoned several times. He introduced the author to English-language poems and literature. Courtesy Tu Tu Tha (*The Irrawaddy*)

In June 2012, I visited the headquarters of the USDP in Naypyidaw, and found to my astonishment that ours were the only vehicles parked in the large compound. We saw office maids lazily cleaning the floors of some near-empty rooms, and only a few officials milling around. Staff members were eager to welcome us. In comparison with the crowded and ramshackle NLD headquarters in Rangoon, the ruling party's offices could accommodate thousands of supporters, but it seemed all had quietly vanished.

While in Naypyidaw I met with former agricultural minister Htay Oo at the party headquarters. The retired general talked at length about what his party had done for the local people: building new roads and buildings, micro-loans, and digging new wells. Like many from a military background, he seemed to be completely out of touch with the reality of modern Burma. He could not comprehend that the NLD could win the

Grand and largely deserted parliament buildings in Naypyidaw

election in 2015. To my astonishment, he also still somehow blindly lived in the past and spoke fondly about his boss, Senior General Than Shwe, and the decision to relocate the capital to Naypyidaw from Rangoon. It was as if Than Shwe had a personality cult similar to North Korea's Kim Jong Il. Htay Oo boasted about often meeting the former junta chief, and I wondered if he really could be so ignorant about how loathed the former dictator is in Burma.

Since my first visit, I have returned to Burma several times. On each occasion I have interviewed political observers, opposition members, and government officials who insist that a landslide NLD victory in Burma's 2015 general election would, in fact, create further difficulties in acheiving national reconciliation. They accuse the NLD of arrogance and of lacking a conciliatory mentality. Some also advised Suu Kyi to abandon the NLD and its elderly leaders and instead become a national figurehead, saying that she should not waste her energy on a party that has become inactive and ineffective under the leadership of the uncles while she was under house arrest. Similarly, many say she should focus on recruiting young and talented advisers, strategists, and economists, and begin to delegate her campaign work to this next generation of activists.

Min Zin, an activist turned political scientist, in a comparison of Suu Kyi and her father, noted that Aung San recruited many talented people to help him lead the nation, asked respected figures to join the cabinet, and enlisted Cambridge-educated Tin Htut to be his chief adviser, as well as delegated to younger followers.

It seems the 2015 general election is there for the taking. However, whether the NLD can evolve into a party of governance as opposed to dissidence, as well as whether they are able to give Burmese people the future they deserve, remain the telling questions.

LOOKING FORWARD

One thing is clear: without the military's cooperation, democracy activists, ethnic groups, and ordinary Burmese will not be able to move forward. They are all fully aware that there is still a long road ahead to reach a free and democratic Burma, and they expect there to be unavoidable setbacks. History has taught Burmese resistance forces to be cautious and ready to make sacrifices, because this current transition to democracy could be revoked at any time.

The vast majority of Burma observers have put the motives behind the junta's transition towards democracy down to self-interest. It is believed by many that the impact of years of punitive international sanctions had begun to take their toll on the military leaders, and that they wanted to escape with the riches they had taken from the country while at the same time making the greatest profit from the assets they still held after sanctions were lifted. Indeed, they were not to be disappointed. By engineering the 2010 general election with a combination of ballot box-stuffing, vote-buying, and blatant intimidation (and even after the generally free and fair by-election in 2012), the USDP of former generals, together with the military quota, control 77 percent of the seats in parliament in one of the most tantalizing nations for investment opportunities in the world.

The benefits of reform have been extraordinary, and Naypyidaw has been far from shy in calling for the rewards of this new "democratic renaissance" to be delivered even more expediently. This is again unsurprising considering the connections the military has with the lucrative Burmese export, telecommunications, and fossil fuels industries.

Many in Burma fear that the military is still pulling the strings behind the new civilian government, and are disgusted that the dictators who ran the country for so many decades remain free to live quiet lives in large compounds in Naypyidaw, as opposed to being held accountable for their brutal actions. It is still a puzzle to many political scientists and observers that senior generals, including Than Shwe, have been able to avoid justice and instead have made a slow and strategic retreat into the background of the political sphere, receiving kudos and a warm embrace from the West for their "progress." For their part, the generals are well aware of the hatred they evoke in Burma, and remain paranoid about being caught and hanged in public. Nevertheless, they have retained enormous wealth and power, and pass their time playing golf and watching politics from behind the scenes.

It seems that the United States and the West consider Suu Kyi robust enough to fight for democracy without their constant support. Nevertheless, unless the constitution is amended, her prospects to take power from the hands of the generals and lead the nation seem slim even if the NLD, as most people expect, wins a landslide in the 2015 general election. Today, people say, Suu Kyi is more than ready to become the president of Burma, even before the 2015 general election. She is aware that her late father General Aung San sacrificed his life for Burma and never had the chance to become leader after the country regained its independence. Her father's colleagues and contemporaries were the ones who experienced power and took control of the country after Aung San was gone. It appears that Suu Kyi wants to finally accomplish her father's mission.

Despite the support that Suu Kyi commands, and her obvious claim to power, it does not appear that the pace of reform will be sufficient to see the military relinquish their enshrined constitutional influence in time for the poll. Those claiming that Burma is on the road to democracy must, therefore, explain how the top generals can be persuaded to relegate themselves to a backseat role.

Many keen observers and critics of Suu Kyi have also questioned Suu Kyi's actions now she is in parliament. They say that she has transformed from a democracy icon into a pragmatic politician with her eye firmly fixed on 2015. She has become silent on the issue of sanctions and is no longer increasing pressure on the generals, or speaking about current and past abuses and allegations of crimes against humanity. Some of her recent decisions have, in fact, harmed those she claims to represent.

In March 2013, a government-appointed commission led by Suu Kyi decided not to close the controversial Chinese-backed Letpadaung copper mine in Sagaing Division, a decision which caused an uproar among Burmese environmental and human rights activists but won applause from influential Chinese investors and officials. A possible motivation for the decision is that the mine's chief investor is the company Wanbao, a subsidiary of China's state-owned arms firm Norinco, and its joint-venture partner is the Union of Myanmar Economic Holdings, a powerful military-owned conglomerate. It appears that if Suu Kyi comes to power after the elections in 2015, Chinese interests will be protected. Another controversial event in March was Suu Kyi's first appearance at the annual Armed Forces Day parade in Naypyidaw. She who historically had been a vocal critic of the armed forces was one of the special guests at the parade, and mingled with generals who are accused of ethnic cleansing, human rights abuses, and large-scale corruption. Shockingly, she even declared in a September 2012 interview that she had a "soft spot" for the generals;[19] a view that does not sit well with many both inside and outside Burma.

Suu Kyi's silence on many burning issues including Chinese-funded mega projects, ethnic bloodshed, and corrupt polititians has shocked many of her former supporters, and it appears that many Burmese have begun to become cynical about the inevitable compromises that have come with her newfound power.

Many in the circle of the regime's dissidents and critics further believe that Suu Kyi is being used or manipulated by the government in order to propitiate the West, particularly the United States, and to encourage them to further ease sanctions and stabilize the often turbulent relationship. If this is the case, the government's strategy has proved to be effective. Those who defend Suu Kyi, however, assert that because her mission is national reconciliation, she has necessarily needed to gain trust and confidence from her former adversaries and the generals who continue to control the power and wealth of the nation. But for all of her compromises, has she persuaded them to respect the rights of the people and to moderate their abusive behavior?

On the border with Thailand and in Western countries, the young Burmese activists and ethnic leaders who vigorously raised awareness and campaigned for the freedom of Suu Kyi, as well as highlighted the plight of those involved inside the movement, have been equally disappointed. Without their dedication and perseverance the Burma cause would be little known. These activists have never sought any political position or reward for their efforts, just a word of recognition and an acknowledgment of their sacrifices by Suu Kyi. They feel that she has betrayed them by her lack of gratitude for their efforts.

Many of those who have long stood behind Suu Kyi—dissidents, activists, and political observers—are belatedly beginning to say that the movement was misguided to focus so much on one individual as an icon of resistance. Many now openly admit that this choice over the past two decades has dealt a great blow to the movement, and that perhaps it is now time to think of a post-Suu Kyi era.

Despite these rumblings of discontent, strangely enough no one has questioned Suu Kyi openly. During my visit to Burma in January 2013, her loyal colleague Win Tin intimated that no one in the party dares question Suu Kyi's authority or provide her with helpful counsel. He felt that Suu Kyi has lost some of her moral leadership, but still enjoys Hollywood-star status. He told me during our meeting in his small living room, "She is hugely popular and she is untouchable." On Suu Kyi's relationship with the government he continued, "She is like a firefighter. They now exploit her status to douse flames and fire whenever they are in crisis." The 1988 Generation group leaders Min Ko Naing and Ko Ko Gyi also do not criticize Suu Kyi openly, but they too intimated during my visit to the former capital that they were sorely disappointed in her leadership. Many former 1988 activists have said that perhaps Suu Kyi became caught up in the wave of the 1988 uprising and did not envision becoming a national leader. It is possible that she simply wanted to work to coordinate and defuse the violence between the socialist regime and the students. Then, inadvertently, the burden of the whole movement fell on her shoulders.

It is interesting to note that despite initially joining the democracy movement as a mediator between the government and the students, Suu Kyi now keeps them at arm's length. It is still a mystery why she does not invite the former student activists to join the NLD. Perhaps she is threatened by the student leaders' popularity in Burma, or perhaps she does not want the honest criticism that they may bring to the NLD.

As for me, I question her personal motives. I wonder whether she spends her time thinking about her next political strategy, about liberating the people of Burma, or about just how best to gain power in 2015.

In these confusing times, and amidst the country's fragile transition, Burma sorely needs a guiding light to provide moral leadership with both conviction and courage. Nevertheless, many remain committed to Suu Kyi and no one is ready to discount her just yet; they have just begun to treat her leadership with healthy skepticism. There is still love and adoration within Burma for The Lady.

What is almost certain despite all the confusion is that the NLD will gain a majority in the next parliament if the election is allowed to take place without the fraudulent activity of 2010. In which case, with the constitution intact, someone in the party other than Suu Kyi will be required to take the helm and lead the nation. Who this would be, at this time, is unclear. This uncertainty, added to the possibility that ethnic rebel groups might lay down their arms and enter the political process—taking near-complete control of some regional assemblies by doing so—could create a political landscape in Burma that is far more diverse than either the generals or the NLD could imagine.

Since the time of Aung San, the opposition movement has transformed dramatically in Burma. But throughout all the decades of opposition, never has freedom been so close at hand. As Suu Kyi reminds us, however, there are still many hills that remain to be climbed, chasms to be bridged, and obstacles to be breached.[20]

The struggle is not over yet.

NOTES

THE LADY

1. Kyaw Zwa Moe, "The Mother Who Was Overlooked," *The Irrawaddy*, July 2006, http://www2.irrawaddy.org/print_article.php?art_id=5945.

2. NLD, "The Brief History of National League for Democracy," Democratic Voice of Burma, nd.

3. Ibid.

4. Aung San Suu Kyi, *Freedom from Fear* 2nd ed. (New York and London: Penguin, 1995), 193.

5. Win Tin, *Bar le ha` lu nga ye* [What's That? A Human Hell?], (Oslo: Democratic Voice of Burma, 2010), 224.

6. "Interview with Aung San Suu Kyi," *Asiaweek*, July 1, 1989, 28.

7. Sutin Wannabovorn, "Suu Kyi's Party Blasts Myanmar Govt on Visa Issue," *Reuters*, March 29, 1999, http://www.burmalibrary.org/reg.burma/archives/199903/msg00638.html.

8. Larry Jagan, "Analysis: Burma's Secret Talks," *BBC News*, March 19, 2002, http://news.bbc.co.uk/2/hi/asia-pacific/1880945.stm.

9. Tony Broadmoor, "The Talks: A Two-Year Chronology," *The Irrawaddy*, February 1, 2004, http://www2.irrawaddy.org/research_show.php?art_id=475.

10. Interview with a senior youth member of the NLD, Chiang Mai, January/February 2011.

11. Tony Broadmoor, "The Talks: A Two-Year Chronology."

12. The Ad Hoc Commission on Depayin Massacre (Burma), "Preliminary Report of the Ad Hoc Commission on Depayin Massacre," (Bangkok: 2004), http://www.burmalibrary.org/docs/Depayin_Massacre.pdf.

13. Peter Popham, *The Lady and the Peacock: The Life of Aung San Suu Kyi of Burma* (UK: Rider, 2012), 357.

14. "Profile: Aung San Suu Kyi Intruder," *BBC News*, August 16, 2009, http://news.bbc.co.uk/2/hi/asia-pacific/8049476.stm.

15. "Suu Kyi to Stand Trial Again Over Unwelcome Visitor," *The Independent*, May 14, 2009, http://www.independent.co.uk/news/world/asia/suu-kyi-to-stand-trial-again-over-us-visitor-1684787.html.

16. Michael Casey, "Monks Put Myanmar Junta in Tight Spot," *Associated Press*, September 22, 2007, http://www.burmanet.org/news/2007/09/22/associated-press-monks-put-myanmar-junta-in-tight-spot-michael-casey/.

17. United Nations, "Human Rights Council 5th Special Session. Resolution S-5/1: Situation of the Human Rights in Myanmar," *Human Rights Council*, October 2, 2007, http://www2.ohchr.org/english/bodies/hrcouncil/docs/specialsession/A.HRC.RES.S.5-1.pdf.

18. Aung Zaw, "Did the NLD Make a Blunder?," *The Irrawaddy*, April 2, 2010, http://www2.irrawaddy.org/print_article.php?art_id=18189.

19. "NLD Says 'No' to Election," *The Irrawaddy*, March 29, 2010, http://election.irrawaddy.org/news/207-nld-says-no-to-election.html.

20. Aung Zaw, "Did the NLD Make a Blunder?"

21. Lalit K Jha, "Generals Resigning for Election May Be Positive: US," *The Irrawaddy*, May 5, 2010, http://election.irrawaddy.org/news/282-generals-resigning-for-election-may-be-positive-us.html.

22. "Myanmar crowds Await Nobel-winner Suu Kyi release," *Associated Press*, November 13, 2010, http://www.aaj.tv/2010/11/myanmar-crowds-await-nobel-winner-suu-kyi-release/.

23. "Supporters, World Leaders Celebrate Suu Kyi Release," *NPR*, November 13, 2010, http://www.npr.org/2010/11/13/131290586myanmar-frees-democracy-advocate-suu-kyi.

24. Ba Kaung, "Suu Kyi Freed at Last," *The Irrawaddy*, November 13, 2010, http://www2.irrawaddy.org/highlight.php?art_id=20068.

25. Interview with Win Tin, September/ October 2010.

26. "Quotes from Aung San Suu Kyi's Press Conference on Sunday," *The Irrawaddy*, November 14, 2010, http://www2.irrawaddy.org/article php?art_id=20084&page=2.

27. Wai Moe, "Suu Kyi to 'First Listen to the People'," *The Irrawaddy*, November 14, 2010, http://www2.irrawaddy.org/print_article.php?art_id=20076.

28. Ibid.

29. Ba Kaung, "Suu Kyi: We Must Strive for Reconciliation," *The Irrawaddy*, November 14, 2010, http://www2.irrawaddy.org/article.php?art_id=20078.

30. "Suu Kyi calls for dialogue with Myanmar government," *CNN*, November 15, 2010, http://articles.cnn.com/2010-11-15/world/myanmar.suu.kyi_1_aung-san-suu-kyi-house-arrest-myanmar?_s=PM:WORLD.

31. John Simpson, "Aung San Suu Kyi Aims for peaceful revolution," *BBC News*, November 15, 2010, http://www.bbc.co.uk/news/world-asia-pacific-11755169.

32. Ibid.

33 Aung Hla Tun and Andrew R. C. Marshall, "Suu Kyi Hails 'Triumph of the People' in Vote Victory," *Reuters*, April 2, 2012, http://in.reuters.com/article/2012/04/02/myanmar-election-suu-kyi-idINDEE83103920120402.

34 Todd Pitman, "Parliament Oath Revision Is Possible: Thein Sein," *The Irrawaddy* April 23, 2012, http://www.irrawaddy.org/archives/2914.

35 Min Zin, "Picking the wrong battle," *Foreign Policy*, April 20, 2012, http://transitions.foreignpolicy.com/posts/2012/04/20/picking_the_wrong_battle.

THE COMRADES

1. "Myanmar Dissident Calls for Change," *New York Times*, November 14, 2010, http://www.nytimes.com/2010/11/15/world/asia/15myanmar.html?_r=0.

2. Hanthawaddy Win Tin, *Hanthawaddy Win Tin and Articles*, (San Francisco: Moe Ma Kha Media, 2008), 34.

3. Telephone conversation with U Win Tin, October 2011.

4. Win Tin, *Bar le ha` lu nga ye* [What's That? A Human Hell?], 224.

5. Hanthawaddy Win Tin, *Hanthawaddy Win Tin and Articles*, 54.

6. Zin Linn, "My Prison Life with U Win Tin," *The Irrawaddy*, April 8, 2001, http://www.irrawaddymedia.com/article.php?art_id=12.

7. Win Tin, *Bar le ha` lu nga ye* [What's That? A Human Hell?], 224.

8. Ibid.

9. Telephone interview with Win Htein, Tin Oo's personal aide, June/ July 2010.

10. Aung San Suu Kyi and Alan Clements, *The Voice of Hope: Conversations with Alan Clements*, (Rider, 2008), 293.

11. Aung Zaw, "A Coup Against Shwe," *The Irrawaddy*, November 24, 2008, http://www2.irrawaddy.org/print_article.php?art_id=14681.

12. Aung San Suu Kyi and Alan Clements, *The Voice of Hope*, 296.

13. "Tin Oo Released," *The Irrawaddy*, February 13, 2010, http://www2.irrawaddy.org/print_article.php?art_id=17913.

14. Aung San Suu Kyi and Alan Clements, *The Voice of Hope*, 296.

15. "US Embassy Cables: Burma's Democracy Movement Being Held Back by 'Uncles'," *The Guardian*, December 9, 2010, http://www.guardian.co.uk/world/us-embassy-cables-documents/161881.

16. Ba Kaung, "NLD Leadership 'Sclerotic': US Embassy," *The Irrawaddy*, December 10, 2010, http://www2.irrawaddy.org/article.php?art_id=20291.

17. Lalit K Jha, "Junta Envoy Says Burma Has No Political Prisoners," *The Irrawaddy*, October 27, 2010. http://election.irrawaddy.org/news/544-junta-envoy-says-burma-has-no-political-prisoners.html.

18. Sai Zom Hseng, "Political Prisoners' Release Remains Uncertain," *The Irrawaddy*, August 26, 2011, http://www2.irrawaddy.org/article.php?art_id=21969.

19. Aung Zaw, "A Spirit That Never Dies," *The Irrawaddy*, October 18, 2011, http://www2.irrawaddy.org/article.php?art_id=22279.

20. "Min Ko Naing: Conqueror of Kings," *Free Min Ko Naing*, http://www.angelfire.com/bc/freemkn/mkn198803.html.

21. Sai Zom Hseng, "Political Prisoners' Release Remains Uncertain."

22. Dominic Faulder, "Fighting a 'Bad King' (Interview/ Min Ko Naing)," *Asiaweek*, October 28, 1988.

23. Interviews with former Burmese political prisoners, 2011.

24. Aung Zaw, "Min Ko Naing, 'Conqueror of Kings'," *The Irrawaddy*, January 1, 2001, http://www2.irrawaddy.org/print_article.php?art_id=3615.

25. Aung Zaw, "Min Ko Naing 'Unsurprised' by His Release," *The Irrawaddy*, November 22, 2004, http://www2.irrawaddy.org/article.php?art_id=4149.

26. Ba Kaung, "Bound and Gagged," *The Irrawaddy*, April 27, 2011, 22.

27. Ibid.

28. Ibid.

29. *The Irrawaddy* Burmese-language website, translated by Aung Zaw, June 9, 2012, http://burma.irrawaddy.org/archives/11701.

30. Htet Aung, "Suu Kyi Starts Networking," *The Irrawaddy*, November 22, 2010, http://www2.irrawaddy.org/article.php?art_id=20148.

31. Wai Moe, "Suu Kyi Listens to Youth," *The Irrawaddy*, December 28, 2010, http://www2.irrawaddy.org/article.php?art_id=20430.

32. Ibid.

33. "Daw Aung San Suu Kyi's Public Address at NLD Headquarters," unofficial translated transcript, *Burma Library*, November 14, 2010, http://www.burmalibrary.org/docs09/DASSK-NLDHQ_speech-2010-11-14.pdf.

34. Aung Zaw, "Burmese Eagerly Await Return of Top Comedian," *The Nation*, June 24, 2007, http://www.aungzaw.net/article_show.php?id=25.

35. Kyaw Zwa Moe, "Putting Compassion into Action," *The Irrawaddy* 16, No. 7 (July 2008).

36. "Farmers Starve In Front of My Eyes," *The Irrawaddy*, August 29, 2011, http://www2.irrawaddy.org/article.php?art_id=21980.

37. Ibid.

38. Ibid.

39. "Lawyer U Aye Myint Given Human Rights Award," *Democratic Voice of Burma*, May 21, 2008, http://www.dvb.no/uncategorized/ lawyer-u-aye-myint-given-human-rights-award/1417.

40. Sai Zom Hseng, "Suu Kyi Factor Helps AIDS Shelters," *The Irrawaddy*, January 13, 2011, http://www2.irrawaddy.org/article.php?art_id=20521.

41. Ibid.

42. Ibid.

43. Alex Ellgee, "Another Birthday behind Bars," *The Irrawaddy*, March 26, 2010, http://www2.irrawaddy.org/article.php?art_id=18128.

44. "Rapping the Regime," *The Irrawaddy* 18, No. 3 (March 2010).

45. "Dissident Hip-Hop Singer Barred from Live Concert," *The Irrawaddy*, August 4, 2011, http://www2.irrawaddy.org/article.php?art_id=21834.

46. Ibid.

47. "Sports Journal Suspended for Suu Kyi Coverage," *The Irrawaddy*, November 19, 2010, http://www2.irrawaddy.org/article.php?art_id=20129.

48. Ibid.

49. Khin Oo Thar, "Suu Kyi Makes Front Page in Burma," *The Irrawaddy*, August 24, 2011, http://www2.irrawaddy.org/article.php?art_id=21951.

50. "New Alliance Designing Joint Union Army," *Shan Herald*, March 2, 2011, http://www.shanland.org/index.php?option=com_content&view=article&id=3491:new-alliance-designing-joint-union-army&catid=85:politics&Itemid=266.

51. Saw Yan Naing, "Ethnic Conflict Key to Rebuilding Nation: Thein Sein," *The Irrawaddy*, July 4, 2012, http://www.irrawaddy.org/archives/8375.

52. Wai Moe, "Suu Kyi: Ready to Help Resolve Ethnic Conflicts," *The Irrawaddy*, July 28, 2011, http://www2.irrawaddy.org/article.php?art_id=21791.

53. Ko Htwe, "Suu Kyi Faces Challenges in Supporting Second Panglong Conference," *The Irrawaddy*, November 22, 2010, http://www2.irrawaddy.org/article.php?art_id=20147.

54. Ibid.

55. "Don't Trivialize the National Cause," *New Light of Myanmar*, December 9, 2010, http://www.burmanet.org/news/2010/12/09/new-light-of-myanmar-don't-trivialize-the-national-cause---banyar-aung/.

56. Ibid.

57. Ibid.

58. Ko Htwe, "Suu Kyi Faces Challenges."

59. "Myanmar's Suu Kyi Makes First Parliament Speech," *The Jakarta Post*, July 25, 2012, http://www.thejakartapost.com/news/2012/07/25/myanmars-suu-kyi-makes-first-parliament-speech.html.

60. "Burma's Suu Kyi Urges Minority Rights," *BBC News*, July 25, 2012, http://www.bbc.co.uk/news/world-asia-18979410.

61. "Suu Kyi Makes First Parliamentary Speech," *Al Jazeera*, July 25, 2012, http://www.aljazeera.com/news/asia-pacific/2012/07/201272585614724337.html.

62. Ibid.

63. Christina Fink, *Living Silence in Burma*.

64. Aung Zaw, "The Power Behind the Robe," *The Irrawaddy* 15, No. 10 (October 2007).

65. Alex Ellgee, "Silencing the Sangha," *The Irrawaddy* 18, No. 11 (November 2010).

66. Ibid.

67. Ibid.

68. Ibid.

69. Aung Zaw, "Engaging Naypyidaw," *The Irrawaddy*, September 25, 2009, http://www2.irrawaddy.org/opinion_story.php?art_id=16862.

70. "Sanctions and the Suu Kyi Syndrome," *The Irrawaddy*, January 19, 2011, http://www2.irrawaddy.org/article.php?art_id=20559&page=1.

71. "Myanmar Parties Join Calls to Lift Sanctions," *AFP*, January 20, 2011, http://www.google.com/hostednews/afp/article/ALeqM5jYPvvVf3dvYkoEcph5KjJjTQdsb g?docId=CNG.92aeb8bdb61f21b28082d7f915770a08.251.

72. "Keep Targeted Sanctions in Place, Says NLD," *The Irrawaddy*, January 17, 2011, http://www2.irrawaddy.org/article.php?art_id=20539.

73. Simon Roughneen, "Burma's Looming Oil/ Gas Auction Could Pit Energy Giants Against Suu Kyi," *The Irrawaddy*, June 21, 2012, http://www.irrawaddy.org/archives/7439.

74. "Barack Obama Sees 'Flickers of Hope' for Democratic Reform in Burma," *The Telegraph* video, 2:01, posted November 18, 2011, http://www.telegraph.co.uk/news/worldnews/asia/burmamyanmar/8898532/Barack-Obama-sees-flickers-of-hope-for-democratic-reform-in-Burma.html.

75. Ibid.

76. Josh Rogin, "Aung San Suu Kyi Initially Opposed Obama's Burma Trip," *Foreign Policy*, November 9, 2012, http://thecable.foreignpolicy.com/posts/2012/11/09/aung_san_suu_kyi_initially_opposed_obama_s_burma_trip.

77. "An Industrial Project That Could Change Myanmar," *New York Times*, November 26, 2010, http://www.nytimes.com/2010/11/27/world/asia/27iht-myanmar.html?pagewanted=all.

78 "Davos 2011: Aung San Suu Kyi Speech in Full," *BBC News*, January 28, 2011, http://www.bbc.co.uk/news/uk-politics-12312254.

79. "UN Officials Welcome Release of Myanmar's Aung San Suu Kyi," *UN News Centre*, November 13, 2010, http://www.un.org/apps/news/story.asp?NewsID=36752#.URMxY6XEO-I.

80. Ibid.

81. "Remarks to the United Nations-ASEAN Ministerial Meeting," *UN News Centre*, September 24, 2010, http://www.un.org/apps/news/infocus/sgspeeches/statments_full.asp?statID=970#.URMyVKXEO-I.

82. Thomas Crampton, "Deal Calls for Security Equipment: UN Envoy's Company Holds Burma Contract," *New York Times*, May 7, 2002, http://www.nytimes.com/2002/05/07/news/07iht-t1_24.html.

83. "United Nations' Burma Envoy Quits," *BBC News*, January 8, 2006, http://news.bbc.co.uk/2/hi/asia-pacific/4592842.stm.

84. Aung Zaw, "Gambari's Mission Is Dead in the Water," *The Irrawaddy*, February 20, 2008, http://www2.irrawaddy.org/opinion_story.php?art_id=10498.

85. "Suu Kyi Refuses to Meet UN Envoy," *The Age*, August 25, 2008, http://www.theage.com.au/world/suu-kyi-refused-to-meet-un-envoy-20080824-41ci.html.

86. Ibid.

87. "Vijay Nambiar Meets Aung San Suu Kyi," *The Hindu*, November 27, 2010, http://www.thehindu.com/news/international/article917635.ece.

88. "Myanmar Gets the Message, UN Says," *UPI*, December 3, 2010, http://www.upi.com/Top_News/Special/2010/12/03/Myanmar-gets-the-message-UN-says/UPI-53861291394155/.

89. "Myanmar Transition Should Include Those Who Did Not Take Part in Polls–UN Envoy," *UN News Centre*, December 2, 2010, http://www.un.org/apps/news/story.asp?NewsID=36940&Cr=myanmar&Cr1#.UPpgzxxi6dg.

90. Lalit K Jha, "Ban Convenes 'Friends of Burma' Meeting," *The Irrawaddy*, September 28, 2010, http://election.irrawaddy.org/news/492-ban-convenes-friends-of-burma-meeting.html.

91. "Burma: Q & A on an International Commission of Inquiry," *Human Rights Watch*, March 24, 2011, http://www.hrw.org/news/2011/03/24/burma-q-international-commission-inquiry.

THE UNFINISHED STRUGGLE

1. Aung Zaw, "Burma's Tightrope," *Foreign Policy*, January 12, 2012, http://www.foreignpolicy.com/articles/2012/01/12/the_tightrope.

2. Andrew R. C. Marshall and Martin Petty, "Myanmar's Thein Sein, Junta Henchman to Radical Reformer," *Reuters*, November 15, 2012, http://www.reuters.com/article/2012/11/15/us-myanmar-theinsein-idUSBRE8AE1RL20121115.

3. Gwen Robinson, "Suu Kyi Misses Opening of Parliament," *Financial Times*, July 4, 2012, http://www.ft.com/intl/cms/s/0/959ae8e4-c57c-11e1-940d-00144feabdc0.html#axzz2KBxMUKtF.

4. "The President's Speech," *The Irrawaddy*, March 2, 2012, http://www2.irrawaddy.org/article.php?art_id=23138.

5. Ibid.

6. "Suu Kyi: Burma Army Could Block Reforms," *CBS News*, January 5, 2012, http://www.cbsnews.com/8301-202_162-57353293suu-kyi-burma-army-could-block-reforms/.

7. David Ljunggren, "Myanmar's Suu Kyi Says Reforms Could Be Reversed," *Reuters*, February 29, 2012, http://www.reuters.com/article/2012/02/29myanmar-suukyi-cabinet-idUSL2E8DT3G720120229.

8. David Wallechinsky, "The Voice of Her People," *Parade Magazine*, January 19, 1997, http://www.guidetoaction.org/magazine/jan97/burma.html.

9. "Aung San Suu Kyi Urges 'Healthy Scepticism' on Burmese Reform," *The Guardian*, June 1, 2012, http://www.guardian.co.uk/world/2012/jun/01/aung-san-suu-kyi-healthy-scepticism.

10. Charlie Campbell, "Thein Sein Blames WEF Absence on Unrest," *The Irrawaddy*, June 8, 2012, http://www.irrawaddy.org/archives/6154.

11. "Aung San Suu Kyi Speaks at Westminster Hall," *UK Foreign & Commonwealth Office*, June 21, 2012, http://www.fco.gov.uk/en/news/latest-news/?view=Speech&id=778619482.

12. David Stringer, "Suu Kyi: Myanmar Headed for Better Future," *The Big Story*, June 21, 2012, http://bigstory.ap.org/article myanmars-suu-kyi-address-british -parliament.

13. "Aung San Suu Kyi Speaks at Westminster Hall," *UK Foreign & Commonwealth Office*, June 21, 2012, http://www.fco.gov.uk/en/news/latest -news/?view=Speech&id=778619482.

14. Ibid.

15. "EU Chief Barroso Offers New Development Aid to Burma," *BBC News*, November 3, 2012, http://www.bbc.co.uk/news/world-asia-20189448.

16. Jocelyn Gecker, "Suu Kyi's Silence on Rohingya Draws Rare Criticism," *The Big Story*, August 16, 2012, http://bigstory.ap.org/article suu-kyis-silence-rohingya-draws-rare-criticism.

17. "Aung San Suu Kyi Aims for Peaceful Revolution," *BBC News*, November 15, 2010, http://www.bbc.co.uk/news/world-asia-pacific-11755169.

18. Hypo Wai Tha, "I Have the Courage to be President," *The Irrawaddy*, October 8, 2012, http://www.irrawaddy.org/archives/15969.

19. Christiane Amanpour, "Interview with Aung San Suu Kyi," CNN, September 21, 2012, transcript.cnn.com/TRANSCRIPT/1209/21/ampr.01.html.

20. David Stringer, "Suu Kyi: Myanmar Headed for Better Future," June 21, 2012, http://bigstory.ap.org/article/myanmars-suu-kyi-address-british-parliament.

INDEX OF NAMES